EX MEX

EX MEX

FROM MIGRANTS TO IMMIGRANTS

JORGE G. CASTAÑEDA

THE NEW PRESS

NEW YORK
LONDON

Requests for permission to reproduce selections from this book should be
mailed to: Permissions Department, The New Press, 38 Greene Street,
New York, NY 10013.

First published in the United States by The New Press, New York, 2007
This paperback edition published by The New Press, New York, 2009
Distributed by Perseus Distribution

ISBN 978-1-59558-455-7 (pbk.)

LIBRARY OF CONGRESS CATALOGING-IN-PUBLICATION DATA

Castañeda, Jorge G., 1953–
    Ex Mex : From migrants to immigrants / Jorge G. Castañeda.
      p. cm.
    Includes bibliographical references and index.
    ISBN 978-1-59558-163-1 (alk. paper) (hc.)
    1. Mexicans—United States.   2. Immigrants—United States.   3. Alien
labor, Mexican—United States.   4. Mexico—Emigration and immigration.
5. United States—Emigration and immigration.   6. Mexico—Emigration
and immigration—Government policy.   7. United States—Emigration and
immigration—Government policy.   8. United States—Relations—Mexico.
9. Mexico—Relations—United States.   I. Title.
E184.M5C368 2008
973.00468'72—dc22

                                                            2007061219

The New Press was established in 1990 as a not-for-profit alternative to the
large, commercial publishing houses currently dominating the book publishing
industry. The New Press operates in the public interest rather than for private
gain, and is committed to publishing, in innovative ways, works of educational,
cultural, and community value that are often deemed insufficiently profitable.

www.thenewpress.com

Composition by NK Graphics, A Black Dot Group Company
This book was set in Fairfield LH Light and Trade Gothic Bold Condensed Twenty

Printed in the United States of America

10   9   8   7   6   5   4   3   2   1

This book is dedicated to the hundreds of Mexican consular officials scattered across the United States whom I had the honor of working with and leading during my tenure as foreign minister, and who selflessly and proudly do their very best, under highly adverse circumstances, to protect and defend our countrymen abroad.

CONTENTS

PREFACE

Before anything else, a few words are in order . . . about what this book is not. I decided against attempting to produce a scholarly treatise on immigration in general, or on Mexican migration to the United States in particular and in recent times. There are far more qualified and prolific academics than I capable of doing so on both sides of the border, and they have done so, over the years. Among them, from different eras, scholars such as Jorge Bustamante (the dean of Mexican "migrationists"), Agustin Escobar, Jorge Durand (actually of Peruvian origin), Victor Zuñiga and Ruben Hernández-León, and others from Mexico, together with Wayne Cornelius, Frank Bean, Douglas Massey, Demetri Papademetriou and Frank Sharry, Jeffrey Passell, Alejandro Portes, Manuel García y Griego, Roberto Suro, and their colleagues in the United States, have done this far better than I could ever hope to. I have tried to benefit from their research, their expertise, and their conclusions, accurately or not, faithfully or not; without their work, this effort would be impossible, but it does not seek to add a great deal of academic knowledge to what they have accomplished, and will continue to achieve.

Concepts such as dispersion or diffusion, circularity and its interruption, quantitative changes becoming qualitative ones, continuity and contiguity, and further theoretical notions mentioned throughout these pages are, needless to say, not of my manufacture. If anything, I simply updated and placed them in a political and binational context. Herein lies the explanation for the virtual absence of footnotes or in-page citations, although every book, essay, article, document, or interview—when possible including an electronic address—is cited in a bibliographical appendix. Whoever wants to know more, or would like to corroborate a fact, statement, or opinion, can do so, while those who just wish to read more comfortably will not be perturbed by the inevitably cumbersome habit of citations, dates, publishers, or references on the page or elsewhere. This is a book for the layman, though I hope the expert will find in it something of use, and, more important, no major misconceptions.

Second, this is not an extended policy paper: what to do, or not to do, in addressing the challenge of migration from Mexico to the United States, and the multiple dilemmas it has wrought for both countries. That is the purpose of the various task-force reports—Mexican, American, and binational, as well as the work of experts and friends such as Frank Sharry, Tamar Jacoby, and Demetri Papademetriou—quoted extensively in this text. They all enjoyed the benefit of resources, pluralism, and versatility that no individual can hope to match; I have only tried to build on the foundations they laid over the past decade or more. Nor is this a journalistic account—anecdotes, vignettes, etc.—of immigration today. Given the currency of the issue in these times, and the reporting talent available in both countries, it would be foolhardy for anyone alien to the profession to dare to intrude on it in this fashion: the reporters' and correspondents' work is quoted and referred to in this book, but the latter is not an effort to rival or replace it. Furthermore, this book does not seek to describe or analyze two of the most recent trends in Mexican migration to the United States: the growing exodus of middle-class professionals from Mexico—doctors, dentists, lawyers, accountants, architects, traders, and executives—to many areas in the United States, from Manhattan to the Twin Cities; and the talent drain, that has led stars from Alejandro González Iñarritu to Salma Hayek, from Alfonso Cuarón to Enrique Norten, from Mario Molina to the late Eduardo Mata, to settle down at least half-time in the United States, where their success is perhaps less difficult to carry than back home. Finally, this is not a memoir by a policy-maker or public figure. I sincerely do not believe my time in office as Mexico's foreign minister, nor what I accomplished in this particular field during my tenure, merits such a title or, indeed, an endeavor of that nature.

Nonetheless, this book does seek to be, partly and modestly, all of the above. Its aim is to provide the reader with an accurate, readable, current, well-informed, and solidly grounded, though fundamentally single-sided, basis for understanding one of the most crucial, controversial, and complex issues in the United States and Mexico today. Single-sided—and I deliberately omit the term one-sided—because it is written from a Mexican perspective, but, unlike many of my previous publishing efforts, at least initially, and in all likelihood exclusively, for a U.S. audience. That is where the debate is raging. In Mexico there is not much disagreement anymore on migration; if anything, as we shall see, there are disputes over details, consequences, tactics, and strategy—not more. But in the course of the vigorous—and on occasion vicious—debate north of the border, it seems to me that the Mexican viewpoint is not always present in the mainstream U.S. discourse. Either because Mexicans in the United States—by definition, the most interested party—do not have access to the ways and means necessary to get their point of view across; or because the Mexican government, after my departure, decided to tone down its decibel level; or because U.S. sympathizers, interpreters, or students of this perspective, regardless of their passion for or affinity with Mexico, inevitably adapt themselves to the context they are immersed in: at the end of the day, it is an American debate. Thus, while this book hopes to be appropriately researched—drawing on the wisdom of the experts and policy-directed—using the encounters and documents I enjoyed the privilege of having access to as a Mexican government official; accessible and descriptive—availing itself of straightforward narrative resources and based upon personal experience—I have been following the migration question in one way or another now for nearly two decades—it should be seen mainly as one more Mexican contribution to the U.S. discussion: not, with false modesty, as an incidental one and certainly not, immodestly, as a definitive one.

Why Mexico? Why immigration? Why now? The three questions are obviously linked, and produce relatively obvious answers. For all practical purposes, the debate in the United States regarding immigration refers to illegal, or unauthorized or undocumented, migration—as we shall see, the terminology is everything but a minor or irrelevant theme—and much less so to the traditional, officially permitted or lawful flows of people from all over the world, frequently well-qualified and educated, and almost always welcomed by a majority of Americans. And unlawful migration is, above all, today, perhaps as it has been now for more than a century, overwhelmingly Mexican. By all accounts, whether one is estimating the flow or the stock, today's numbers or yesterday's, conservative projections or doomsday scenarios, between half and two-thirds of any figure one chooses is Mexican. There are roughly 12 million unauthorized non-American-born individuals currently in the United States; at least 6 million are Mexican; every year around half a million people enter the United States without papers; at least 350,000 to 400,000 are Mexican. And a similar proportion emerges from the "legal" numbers, or from the historic ones: Latino or Hispanic heritage in the United States means, more than ever, Mexican. The flow of Cubans, Puerto Ricans, and Central Americans is drying up, and other Latin Americans, for now at least, cannot match the Mexican exception.

But if, from this perspective, immigration in the United States is about Mexico, it is also a central issue for Mexico, and the foremost one on its agenda with the neighbor to the north. Today approximately 11 percent of the country's population— i.e., people born in Mexico and remaining Mexican citizens— reside in the United States. This is much less than Ecuador (18 percent of the population, according to a possibly exaggerated estimate by its Central Bank) or El Salvador (25 percent, according to its president in 2005), but slightly more than the Philippines (one of the few countries that have guest-worker programs with other nations); significantly more than Morocco (8 percent, which also has guest-worker programs), and Turkey (9 percent, which has signed them in the past). The number of Mexicans with family in the United States and of Mexicans who would travel to work abroad if they could, the amount of money those who do send back each month, and the self-perpetuating nature of the current demographic and migratory status quo—all point in the same direction: this issue will be increasingly important for Mexico and the U.S. relationship with Mexico, at least for another decade. Then, perhaps, if Mexico's economy continues to grow at least as it has done the past twelve years (around 3 percent yearly, on average), and

given the rapid aging of its population and the subsequent reduction in the pool of potential emigrants, things may settle
down, and a steady state may be achieved. But not before, and
thus the debate will continue to smolder in the United States
for some time. So now is the time to place one's five cents'
worth, even if only from a vantage point that the United States
has never held in high regard: what the rest of the world thinks.

This is essentially a descriptive text, which seeks to explain,
rather than to advocate solutions or formulate proposals. It
would be an abdication of responsibility and intellectual hon-
esty, however, not to suggest, in the concluding chapter, a number of ideas that would fit in the logical evolution of Mexican
immigration to the United States, and that at the same time
would address the multiple concerns the issue entails. These
ideas do not constitute a silver bullet, they are not necessarily
politically correct, and they may even seem illusory or unfeasible for now. On the other hand, they may point in the right direction, which is perhaps all one can ask of ideas in relation to
a question of this complexity.

I have received large doses of help, advice, and support
from many friends in the course of this book's writing. I am
grateful to: my initial research assistants, Eva Gurría, Eric Fabila,
and Jessica Berdejo for their willingness to work on a project
that was hard to visualize; Gustavo Mohar, my former chief negotiator on immigration issues and currently deputy chief of
Mexico's Intelligence and Security Agency, for the friendship,
insights, documents, and patience he shared with me; Javier
Barros, for having indirectly suggested the title; Douglas Massey,
who corrected many—but inevitably not all—of my simplistic
views of Mexican immigration; Jorge Bustamante, Andrés Rozental, Andrea Oñate, and Cassio Luiselli, who read the manuscript;
Alejandra Zerecero and Mariana Celorio, my two personal as-

sistants who make my life possible; and lastly, to Edurne Ponce de León Tazón, who was much more than a research assistant: a magician who managed to find everything I asked her for, correct every mistake she found, substantiate every unfounded claim, and be infinitely tolerant and good-natured. And of course, to André Schiffrin, who in his wisdom has discovered how to be a friend, an editor, and a critic, all at the same time.

EX MEX

ONE

Every night at 1:55 A.M., fifty to one hundred some-odd Mexicans from the state of Puebla board the Mexicana Airlines redeye from John F. Kennedy International Airport to Mexico City. The other passengers, who have waited half the night to take Mexicana's only direct flight from New York to the Mexican capital, brace themselves for the worst kind of flight: too long to just read or watch the movie; too short to get a good night's sleep before arrival at six o'clock in the morning. They wonder why in the world the airline decided to schedule its flight this way. Why not just leave in the late afternoon, like before, and arrive in the late evening, like before? Those passengers have of course no way of ascertaining the reasons that led Mexicana executives, just before their company's privatization, to revamp the JFK schedules to favor their most important customers: the *paisanos*, or migrants, going home to Puebla to visit the family.

It turns out those customers had complained about the previous flight times. They would arrive at Benito Juárez International Airport in Mexico City late at night, no longer able to catch the last two-hour bus ride to Puebla de los Angeles, the capital of their state, from where they would head up to the sierra, or to Tehuacán in the lowlands, or elsewhere in the Mixteca region, from where nearly half a million Mexicans currently living and working in the tristate area come from. So they would have to pass the night at one of the seedy, dangerous flophouses around the airport, needlessly spending wages hard-earned on the streets of Manhattan, risking holdups by petty thieves, shakedowns by the police, or express kidnappings by professional criminals. Thus, their complaint to Mexicana: save us the hotel, let us work the day in New York, get some sleep on the plane, and be on our way to Puebla at dawn the next morning. The airline complied, put new Airbus 320 jetliners on its route, and everyone, except a smattering of business executives in first class, was happy.

An unscientific but revealing sample of the passengers collected over several days highlighted various facts about Mexicans in New York who fly back and forth regularly. They are not all migrants: many are actually couriers, lugging things—of every imaginable sort: letters, money, food, secondhand clothes, artifacts—to and from New York to their hometowns. But many—a majority—are migrants, and they practically all come from the central state of Puebla. They are mostly permanent residents, they say they speak English, a thin majority would like to become U.S. citizens; they all send money back to Mexico, and most work in the restaurant business. The airline flight plan reflects the constantly evolving reality of Mexican immigration to New York and elsewhere in the United States, as well as changing Mexican attitudes about it. For the record, suffice it to say that Mexicana 001 is not unique: there are, on average, ninety flights per day from Mexico City to the United States; forty-three from Guadalajara; seventeen from León-El Bajío; three from Puebla; and two from Zacatecas. None of these are tourist destinations, though a significant share of the passengers to the capital and Guadalajara are either business-linked, or in-transit visitors to tourist spots.

The first lesson from Mexicana 001 involves and debunks the myth of illegality. Every passenger on the red-eye is legal: they could not get on the plane without a passport and I-94 form stapled to it, and the latter can only be obtained when entering the United States with a valid visa. Obviously, a large proportion of Mexicans in New York are not legal; but those on the plane are, and they are numerous. Moreover, and more important, none of the passengers would consider going home for whatever reason, without the absolute certainty of being able to return; because ever since President Bill Clinton decided to clamp down on immigration in 1996 by building walls and complicating entry to the United States, what the experts call circularity was interrupted. People who for years had been coming and going between the two countries, with or without papers, decided it was time to settle down, north of the harder-to-cross border. They gave up seasonal migration, brought the family up when possible and affordable, and hunkered down till they became legal, one way or another. Everyone on Flight 001 has papers; no one could or would board it without them. This represents a major transformation in relations between the two countries: for more than a century immigration from Mexico to the United States had been characterized by this circularity, or seasonality.

A second sea change exemplified by Flight 001 involves New York City, and more generally, the extension of Mexican immigration to nearly everywhere in the United States. Just twenty years ago, New York was everything but a Mexican town. Dominicans—and of course Puerto Ricans since the 1950s—were the predominant Latinos or Hispanics in the city. Small groups of Mexicans had found work in Yonkers and New Rochelle, but by and large there were no *poblanos* in the area's flower shops, grocery stores, restaurants, and construction sites. Paradoxically, the people from Puebla were key allies for the

Korean takeover of New York's mom-and-pop stores. Today, there are, by most accounts, upwards of half a million Mexicans in the whole region—a recent, insightful study by Robert Courtney Smith, *Mexican New York*, estimates between 700,000 and 750,000—and New York City, all boroughs included, is rapidly becoming a town where Mexican immigrants are as omnipresent and distinguishable as their fellow Latinos. Two-thirds of those Mexican migrants come from the Mixteca region, an area composed mainly of chunks of the states of Puebla, Oaxaca, and to a lesser extent Guerrero. These impoverished, barren sierras of southeastern Mexico have been all but emptied of their inhabitants over the past twenty years, though they had not traditionally been a "sending" region, that is, an area of the country where for generations young men have been "heading north" as a virtual rite of passage. According to Courtney Smith, 70 percent of the departures have been to New York.

This helps explain another strange feature of Mexicana's Flight 001, a reflection of the recent evolution of Mexican society toward much greater access for many more people to consumer goods and services and to middle-class economic levels, though not necessarily social status. The passengers of Flight 001, unlike those of other flights to Mexico City earlier in the day, or to or from other destinations in Mexico, look unmistakably like the stereotype Mexicans are supposed to look like. In similar fashion to the newly arrived guests at middle-class, all-inclusive resorts in Acapulco or Puerto Vallarta, or at the World Cup Soccer Championship held in Germany in 2006—where Mexico's games were attended by 35,000 Mexican tourists, according to some calculations—those passengers no longer have the traditional, Mexican, upper-middle-class appearance on these flights: light-skinned, tall, thin, and elegantly, or at least fashionably, dressed, middle-aged or just married. The coach passengers on

Mexicana 001 are dark-skinned; short; with countless children; loaded with shopping bags, packages, gifts, and their own snacks or meals; and colorfully but informally dressed. Together, they resemble a gathering in a Mexico City street market (or *tianguis*) rather than travelers on an international flight that costs well over $500 round-trip. The Mexican middle class is finally beginning to look . . . Mexican. Except that unlike its earlier members, who climbed the social ladder over the course of more than half a century, and more or less simultaneously attained the corresponding educational, cultural, and societal accoutrements, fortunately the migrants—as well as their families back home—have made the jump in a much shorter period of time. So their educational levels and social skills have not quite kept up with their rapid economic graduation. The most revealing factoid may be the following: according to one of its owners, 45 percent of the passengers on Mexico's new, low-cost airline, Volaris, are first-time flyers—an astonishing figure. This explains the tianguis in the sky, on the beach, or in Dortmund, Germany: immigration and twelve years of economic stability and relative prosperity under presidents Ernesto Zedillo, Vicente Fox, and Felipe Calderón have created a new Mexican middle class that doesn't quite look or act the role, but that has become one of the country's best kept secrets and most sacred treasures. It is the single most important factor in the beginning of a reduction in ancestral Mexican inequality.

The transformation of Mexican New York has occurred in the space of two decades, and in a similar vein to what has happened in so many other places in the United States, from Miami to the Carolinas, from Iowa to Detroit, from Las Vegas to Indianapolis. The mutations whose description follows were detected in the specialized literature between five and ten years ago, although they only acquired their current dimensions in very recent times. Among the precursors from 2001 or earlier that deserve to be mentioned are Wayne A. Cornelius and Enrico A. Marcelli, "The Changing Profile of Mexican Migrants to the United States: New Evidence from California and Mexico," *Latin American Research Review* 36, no. 3 (2001); Jorge Durand, Douglas S. Massey, and Rene M. Zenteno, "Mexican Immigration to the United States: Continuities and Changes," *Latin American Research Review* 36, no. 1 (2001); and, most recently and most specifically, Victor Zuñiga and Rubén Hérnandez-Leon, *New Destinations: Mexican Immigration in the United States*, with data through the year 2000. In 2005 there were, according to the most recent statistics from the United States Bureau of the Census (BOC), that do not include prison, hospital, or university populations (which in the Mexican case would not change much), 10,826,766 Mexican-born individuals in the United States, more people than live in the Federal District, Mexico's humongous capital. This represented a 20 percent increase over 2000, and roughly six times as many as the next nationality, the Chinese. The total includes, of course, those with papers and without them, as well as naturalized Americans, i.e., Mexican-born U.S. citizens. The breakdown into these sub-categories is a bit more difficult to arrive at, since the classification carried out by the BOC does not specify legal status. But by other accounts, approximately 14 percent of this total corresponds to naturalized Americans, 53 percent to unauthorized immigrants, and 33 percent to permanent legal residents.

The numbers also—and perhaps more revealingly—showed how immigration from Mexico can now be classified into three groups, as described in a long, front-page article published in the August 15, 2006, *New York Times*, when the numbers were made available. The first involves the traditional gateway states for all immigrants: California, New York, Texas, Florida, New

Jersey, and Illinois. The growth rates in these states were about the same as the national average for the period in question. In fact, dispersion or diffusion essentially means the movement away from California, and, to a lesser extent, Texas as the main destinations for Mexican migrants. According to Jorge Durand, Douglas Massey, and Chiara Capoferro in *New Destinations*, five factors deflected immigration away from California in the second half of the 1990s:

a sharp increase in the costs and risks of border-crossing in the San Diego area; a slow-down of the California economy; the emergence of an strong anti-immigration sentiment in the state (exemplified by Governor Pete Wilson's support of Proposition 187 to promote his reelection in 1994); the mobility many migrants obtained through the amnesty and legalization process that took place between 1987 and 1992; and finally the economic boom across the United States from 1992 onward.

This movement was directed fundamentally toward the so-called second-tier states, where immigrants from Mexico tend increasingly to settle after initially showing up in the gateway states. These, according to the previously quoted *Times* article, include North Carolina, Georgia, Washington, and Massachussetts, among others. But a new set of so-called "third-tier" states has emerged, where extremely fast-growing settlements of Mexicans have sprung up in the last decade or less, including people who arrive there directly from Mexico, without sojourning for a couple of years in the traditional destinations. The increases in the number of Mexican-born individuals in these states were among the highest in the entire United States, well above the national average: South Dakota, 44 percent;

Delaware, 32 percent; Missouri, 31 percent; New Hampshire, 26 percent; Indiana, 34 percent.

This last state, along with Minnesota, for example, witnessed such a strong increase that the Mexican government found itself obliged to open new consulates in Indianapolis and Minneapolis/St. Paul, adding to the forty-seven consular offices Mexico already has in the United States, the largest by far of any country in the world. Similarly, in 2001, when the Mexican Foreign Ministry considered opening a new consulate in Las Vegas, and was strongly urged to do so by Nevada Senator and now Democratic Majority Leader Harry Reid, it discovered that by some estimates there were up to 700,000 Mexicans without papers in the city, toiling in the hotels, restaurants, casino kitchens, and parking lots. In the 1980s the only Mexicans in Las Vegas were mariachi singers and the high-rolling gamblers padding the profits of casino owners and croupiers at the roulette wheels. In all, the dispersion is almost beyond belief: according to an NPR/Kaiser/Kennedy School poll conducted throughout the United States in mid-2004, 71 percent of respondents said there were at least some "illegal immigrants" in their communities. This newness initially generates a backlash, but later, attitudes change. As the Harvard University Press *Guide to Immigration since 1965* states: "Native-born Americans who interact with immigrants frequently tend to have more positive opinions of them than those who do not. . . . A consistent finding in public opinion polls is that exposure to and experience with immigrants leads to greater acceptance of them."

An even better example than Las Vegas is a small Ohio community I visited in 2006: Middletown, where Miami University of Ohio has one of its three campuses. It's a town of 60,000 people, located in Butler County, not far from Dayton. The main economic activity remains the steel mill, bought some years back by Kawasaki Steel, from Japan; otherwise it's a plain, unexceptional mid-American community. One change has occurred though, in the last ten years: approximately 1,000 Mexicans now live and work there, coming literally out of nowhere, to the middle of nowhere; in Butler County as a whole, from 2000 to 2005, the Hispanic population rose 56 percent. The new residents work in landscaping, a packaging plant, some hospitals, construction, garbage processing, and other similar service industries. They don't make much: including overtime, maybe $9 or $10 an hour (still, well above the probable average for undocumented Mexicans), and have begun to create their own businesses, attending to their own needs and tastes. Like Mexicans across the United States, they are hardworking, squeaky-clean honest, and largely lacking papers, having paid between $1,700 and $3,000 to a smuggler for guiding them to their destination, mostly the home of a family member who staked them for that sum. Many, though not all, are now married with children in the United States.

The difference between Middletown and hundreds of other communities throughout the United States today, and their reality a decade or two ago, is the newness of Mexicans, and the backlash their presence has begun to unleash. Sheriff Richard Jones of Butler County has threatened to arrest them, as well as people who employ them, and spews racist rhetoric for the local media day in and day out; the Motor Vehicle Bureau has begun requesting proof of citizenship for licenses; businesses such as construction and landscaping contractors are becoming wary of hiring Mexicans; the Mexicans are frightened by their neighbors; and their neighbors are scared of them. Jones is unabashed; the sheriff's office has posted a Web call saying: "If you know of any persons you feel are here illegally, or know of an employer who regularly hires illegal aliens, please contact the Butler County sheriff's office with any information you feel will help us rid Butler County of this financial burden." Butler reproduces conservative Republican views: according to national polls, they are almost twice as likely as liberal Democrats to favor denying illegal aliens basic social services, and though they approve of giving their children education, they do so by ten points less than the national average and twenty points less than liberal Democrats. The ideological right does not like immigration, though the business community does. With time, Butler's hysteria and conservatives' opposition will probably pass, as similar attitudes have faded in the past; but for now, Middletown is experiencing a totally unfathomed experience: people from another world suddenly living and working next door. It's difficult, as it also is for the other side of the political spectrum.

Indeed, Mexicans are slammed from the left too, particularly in parts of the African American leadership and community. Despite calls from leaders such as Jesse Jackson to the effect that immigrants and blacks should be allies, other African American leaders or scholars see competition and rivalry. Many of them believe that Mexican immigrants compete directly for jobs with blacks, driving down wages and working conditions because of their "illegal" nature. Thus, Frank Morris, a former director of the Congressional Black Caucus Foundation, stated in 2006 that "as long as there is an available labor supply, [immigrants] will be preferred to African Americans. Employers prefer illegal immigrants because they can be exploited without any recourse." And, in fact, the occupational distribution of Latinos resembles the profile of black workers most closely, with similar proportions of both to be found in professional services, sales, and production occupations. As is now relatively well known, many progressives oppose a guest-worker program, for example, because they believe it would increase the risks that Mexicans without papers would either take away jobs from blacks, or drive down their wages through unfair competition. The experts, as usual, disagree among themselves. Bernard Anderson, an economist and professor at the Wharton School of the University of Pennsylvania, says blaming high black unemployment on immigrant workers is unfair: "The immigrant presence in the American labor market has not had a major detrimental effect on the wages and employment of African American workers; there isn't any statistical evidence to back up the talk of immigrants 'stealing' jobs from blacks. Most of it is based on observation and anecdotes. It's not based on systematic research; either black workers have left the labor market altogether or black workers have moved on to other jobs that pay more or pay the same." Conversely, a 2004 study by George J. Borjas, a Harvard University professor of economics and social policy, presents a contrary picture: "Although the 1980–2000 immigrant influx lowered the wage of white workers by 3.5 percent and of Asians by only 3.1 percent, it reduced the wage of blacks by 4.5 percent and that of Hispanics by 5.0 percent. The adverse impact of immigration, therefore, is largest for the most disadvantaged native-born minorities."

This is not necessarily true everywhere in the United States, nor at all wage or skill levels, but can be accurate in given cities (Los Angeles, for example) and in certain sectors—the low-wage, low-skill jobs that many Mexicans fill. The African American population is sympathetic to the immigrant cause, and can harbor favorable views of immigrants, but clearly is more concerned than whites about job implications. According to a Pew Hispanic Research Survey carried out in April 2006, blacks in the general public are more supportive than whites of permitting illegal immigrants to stay in the United States. About half say they should be allowed to stay, while an identical percentage of blacks believes illegal immigrants should be sent home; the equivalent percentage for whites is 59 percent vs. 33 percent. However, more blacks than whites say they or a family member have lost a job, or not gotten a job, because an employer hired an immigrant worker (22 percent vs. 14 percent); blacks are also more likely than whites to feel that immigrants take jobs away from U.S. citizens rather than take jobs that Americans don't want (34 percent vs. 25 percent). But in the overall assessment, one would have to take into account how many blacks' and other minorities' jobs cheap Mexican labor has *saved* the United States by making it more competitive in the face of the Chinese—and to a lesser extent Indian—onslaught. Never, perhaps, in economic history, has there been such a pronounced change in the relative price of labor in the world, than through the globalization of the Chinese and Indian work force. This entire discussion must also be seen in that light.

So Mexicans in more places in the United States are changing U.S. attitude, but Mexicans from more places in Mexico are changing Mexican attitudes. The American metamorphosis reflects another deep transformation, this time in Mexico, but mirroring the one in the United States: the extension of the out-migration phenomenon from four Mexican states to almost all of them. For decades, nearly three-quarters of Mexican migrants in the United States originated in the rural areas of the states of Jalisco, Guanajuato, Michoacán, and Zacatecas, the first three being deeply religious, conservative, and poor states in the central region of the country known as El Bajío; Zacatecas is a mining state on the dividing line between Mexico's center and the north. But by the 1980s at the latest, immigration trends began to change dramatically, with outflows commencing elsewhere in the country: from Hidalgo and Morelos, close to Mexico City, the nation's capital; from Oaxaca, Guerrero, and Puebla,

in the country's poor southeast; from Chiapas along the border
with Guatemala; from Veracruz, along the Gulf Coast; and, inevitably, from Mexico City, and the surrounding state of Mexico.
Joe Contreras, *Newsweek*'s chief Latin American correspondent,
recalls a telling anecdote in his recent book on Mexico and the
United States, when he accompanied me on a campaign swing
through Acapulco, where in the 1950s American starlets showed
their wares and plied their trade, and in the 1970s American
couples like Hillary and Bill Clinton enjoyed their honeymoons.
At an evening town hall meeting with a few hundred locals in
2004, my interlocutors and I asked everyone in the small crowd
to raise their hands if they had family in the United States;
practically everybody did. This, in a large, relatively prosperous
city, the business center of a state that had never sent people
north. Similar reactions emerged in countless other town meetings along the Pacific Coast, in Chiapas, and even in Yucatán.

There is a paradox here: the reactions just cited above, in
Ohio and Acapulco, are partly compatible with the real statis-
tics on immigration, but not entirely. Although Mexicans from
more regions of their country are *departing* to more regions of the
United States than ever before, there are not that many more
Mexicans *emigrating* to the United States today than before.
The best guess for current total yearly immigration from Mexico, legal and not legal, is around 400,000. During the 1942–64
Bracero or Temporary Worker Program, set up between the two
countries for the World War II war industry and agriculture,
4.2 million Mexicans entered the United States for specific periods of time, coming and going from Mexico: a yearly average
of about 200,000 legal seasonal workers. To this figure—and for
the 1942–64 period—we can add about 25,000 average yearly
legal, permanent immigrants, and perhaps 150,000 unauthorized ones. In his book *Los Mojados: The Wetback Story*, Julian

Samora estimates that by the end of the program, the number of braceros was about the same as the number of undocumented workers. The sum is only slightly lower than today. Thus the *flow* has not changed much, but, from 1986 onward, the *stock* began to rise substantially. Indeed, the above-mentioned numbers for the 1942–64 period are for a time when the population of Mexico ranged from 20 million to 35 million; today, with the same flow, the population has reached 110 million.

Here are the numbers, as best as they can be estimated.* In 1920, there were 486,000 Mexican-born persons in the United States, legal and not legal, though the distinction was then ambiguous, at best: 3.4 percent of Mexico's population and 0.45 percent of the American one. In 1930, 641,000 Mexican-born individuals were present in the United States: 3.8 percent of Mexico's population and 0.52 percent of U.S. inhabitants. In 1940, the equivalent numbers, much lower owing to the Depression and the fact that World War II and the Bracero Agreement had not yet begun, were 377,000, that is, 1.9 percent of Mexico's population and 0.3 percent of the U.S. population. By 1950, the numbers increased, but not by much, since the Bracero Agreement provided for intensive circularity or seasonality. People could come and go legally with great ease and did: 450,000, in other words, 1.7 percent of Mexico's population, which was by then growing at a breakneck pace, and 0.3 percent of the U.S. population. In 1960, as the Bracero Agreement was winding down, the figure for Mexican-born inhabitants north of the border was 575,000, or 1.6 percent of Mexico's to-

*This is according to the NATLHIST database from the *Mexican Migration Project*, developed by the Research Department of Social Movements at the University of Guadalajara and the Office of Population Research at Princeton University (http://mmp.opr.princeton.edu/data bases/supplementaldata-en.aspx).

tal and 0.3 percent of the U.S. total. The 1970 numbers confirmed the stability of the numbers: 760,000 in the United States, or 1.6 percent of Mexico's inhabitants and 0.4 percent of the U.S. population. The stability is all the more striking when one recalls that these were simultaneously the golden years of Mexico's economic boom and population explosion.

But by 1980, the statistics had begun to increase drastically; the end of the Bracero era reduced circularity, though it did not eliminate it, and in 1976 Mexico went through its first serious economic crisis in three decades. Thus, there were now 2.2 million Mexicans abroad, the equivalent of 3.16 percent of Mexico's population and almost 1 percent of the U.S. total. In 1990, after Ronald Reagan's amnesty of 1986, the population reached 4.3 million, or 5.3 percent of all Mexicans, and 1.7 percent of the American total. In 2000, as a direct result of the end of circularity—perhaps the most important change ever in real-life U.S. immigration policy toward Mexico—the total had surged to 9.2 million, or 9.4 percent of the Mexican population and 3.2 percent of the U.S. total. By 2005, the last numbers available, roughly 11 million Mexican-born individuals lived in the United States, which amounted to 11 percent of the Mexican population, now growing very slowly and rapidly aging, and 3.8 percent of the U.S. total. The changes that took place from 1986 onward explain—though they cannot justify—reactions like Sheriff Richard Jones's, from Butler County.

These numbers also help to explain, of course, the behavior of Mexican businesses like Mexicana Airlines. With 11 million potential customers in the United States, one listens and accommodates. Yet perhaps the most telling implication of Mexicana Airlines' decision to placate its best customers is of a deeper, more intangible sort. For many years, indeed until quite recently, Mexican business and Mexicans in general paid no heed to their compatriots abroad. At best they ignored them; at worst, they looked down on them for bailing out from their troubled land. They were seen as deserters, turncoats, or weaklings, unable or unwilling to stick it out back home. The attitude never made any sense, obviously; people left because jobs at home were either unavailable or poorly paid, and because their parents had been emigrating for decades; many of those who did depart came home regularly; they all sent money back to their families and communities; and more significantly, most of the time, the emigrants were their regions' or homes' "best and brightest": the most adventuresome, the most entrepreneurial, the boldest. Still, as early as 1920, the Catholic Church of Jalisco, one of the first and largest sending states, made quite clear its thoughts on the matter: "[The migrants'] separation from the country contributes to the decadence of the fatherland. . . . Leaving their country in the difficult straits it finds itself in, is anti-patriotic. . . . Their lack of patriotism is even greater when one recalls that they are going off to work, and consequently to contribute with their work, to the greatness of a nation that has considered itself an enemy of ours and has been responsible for our greatest national disasters." And later, in the 1930s, just after the Mexican Revolution, the government itself would claim that emigration "was bleeding Mexico white"; according to David Fitzgerald, a University of California at San Diego scholar, "Discourses about the bleeding of Mexico to gringo advantage reflected a period of intensive state-led nationalizing." So neither from right nor left, did Mexicans like emigration and emigrants.

All of this began to evolve in the late 1980s and early 1990s, when on the one hand underlying trends in Mexican migration—described by many of the scholars cited in the bibliographical appendix—started taking hold, and on the other the government's approach also underwent a significant shift. The extension of the traditional concentration of the migrants from the four above-mentioned states to other regions; the shift from purely rural sending areas to increasingly urban ones; the slow but sure closing of the gender gap, as more and more women began to leave alone, or accompanying their partners: all of these changes generated a major transformation of the entire migration process and Mexican attitudes in its regard. According to some estimates, until 2000, women represented less than 45 percent of the stock, or total Mexican population living in the United States, and about the same percentage, perhaps a bit less, of the yearly flow north. These numbers have remained relatively constant over recent years, but other mutations are important, starting with absolute numbers: there are now about 5 million Mexican-born women in the United States, of which about 2.5 million are unauthorized. In addition, it seems that there is a rising number of women who come alone; second, they are different, sociologically, from male migrants. Those who began to try their luck on their own, north of the border, in the early 1990s, were mostly between twelve and twenty-four years of age, that is, on average about six years younger than their male counterparts, with a slightly higher educational level than the latter. They tended to be more urban, more from the north of Mexico, and to find work more easily, but earned about 30 percent less than men did.

As emigration spread throughout the country and across gender lines, a growing number of Mexicans from every walk of life and every state in the nation began to enter into contact with migrants. It is much more difficult to blame and badmouth your cousin, *compadre*, or *novio* for leaving, than to do so about abstract strangers. Similarly, educational levels improved: from poor peasants under the Bracero Program, between 1942 and 1965, emigration as the twentieth century came to an end included more and more young, middle- or high-school students from the cities, wearing tennis shoes instead of boots or *guaraches*, baseball caps instead of sombreros. These changes were picked up by many students of the issue, even unspecialized ones like myself; as early as 1993, in "The Paradox of Tolerance and Dedemocratization" (Abraham F. Lowenthal and Katrina Burgess, eds., *The California-Mexico Connection*, Stanford University Press, 1993), I emphasized the cultural impact of these transformations for small, rural, conservative communities in the sending regions.

Most important, the money they were sending home began to be counted, and counted upon. The first semiofficial attempt to tabulate remittances occurred in 1980; a study carried out on a personal basis by a Central Bank official estimated that undocumented migrants had, in 1975, sent back roughly half a billion dollars. This was much less than other experts surmised (Wayne Cornelius, then of MIT, now at the University of California at San Diego, and one of the leading U.S. immigration experts, guessed between $2 billion and $3 billion a bit before; see Jorge Durand and Douglas S. Massey's "Mexican Migration to the United States: A Critical Review"), and also left out remittances by documented Mexicans, on the premise that they transferred less money than those with papers. The figure was the first serious one, but not sufficiently accurate, almost certainly guilty of undercounting. Until 1989, the Central Bank only calculated postal and wire transfers, and so did not really possess any official, complete tally. But beginning in 1989, it included money orders and personal checks moving through the banking system. Between 1989 and 1992 total remittances, added up this way, grew from $1.7 billion to $3 billion. From 1992 onward the numbers became much more reliable, and a new, additional statistical correction was applied in 1999. Remittances grew from the $3.5 billion range through 1996 to $6.5 billion in 2000, $10 billion in 2002, $13 billion in 2003, $16 billion in 2004, $20 billion in 2005, and $23 billion in 2006. The evolution of the total probably reflects three trends: more people, sending more money, that is more accurately tabulated; it remains, however, hard to explain. That said, it is useful to place all of this in perspective. Remittances today represent roughly 2.5 percent of Mexico's GDP; much less than any other Latin American country (El Salvador, the Dominican Republic, and Ecuador stand way over 10 percent), not to mention Eastern European countries, or former Soviet Union republics, for example, ranging from 27 percent for Moldova to 5 percent for Hungary, and including 12 percent for Serbia, 10 percent for Armenia, and 7 percent for Georgia.

This led successive Mexican governments in the late 1980s and 1990s, who needed this money badly but were also sensitive to the other changes under way, to adopt a new approach to migrants, particularly after the 1988 presidential elections. In those elections, Cuauhtémoc Cárdenas, former governor of Michoacán and son of Lázaro Cárdenas, the country's revered president of the 1930s, mounted the most serious challenge ever to the existing one-party system that had dominated Mexico's politics since the founding of the Partido Revolucionario Institucional or Institutional Revolutionary Party (PRI) in 1929. Carlos Salinas de Gortari, the PRI candidate, may have actually lost the election and became acutely aware that in any case he had certainly been defeated in the battle for the hearts and minds of his compatriots in the United States, among other reasons because his rival originated, like so many migrants, from the state of Michoacán. On taking office, the new government rapidly reached out to communities north of the border, establishing a more modern and outward-looking consular system, inviting Latino leaders to Mexico City, and in general transforming official Mexican views of migrants: no longer despised, they quickly mutated to potential allies or, at least, friends. In the early 1990s, the Mexican Foreign Ministry even established a Mexican Communities Program to address their needs and concerns.

A similar but more important alteration took place under the next and last PRI president, Ernesto Zedillo, elected in what was probably the country's first free—if not totally fair—election in 1994. Two years later, he finally owned up to what myriad Mexicans had known for decades: innumerable border residents held both Mexican and American citizenship since time immemorial, and hundreds of thousands of Mexicans—and perhaps millions—whose presence in the United States had been legalized under the amnesty provisions of the 1986 Immigration Reform and Control Act (IRCA), would soon be applying for American citizenship, without wanting to lose their Mexican nationality. The ballpark figure for total legalizations of Mexicans as a result of IRCA, including the so-called Special Agricultural Workers (SAWs), as well as family reunifications, was well over 3 million (1.3 million through amnesty, 1.1 million as SAWs, and at least another million through subsequent family reunifications in the out years). This process occurred over a ten-year period (five years of temporary residence and five years of permanent residence), and it is not easy to separate the number of legalizations that took place during this period as a result of IRCA from those that would have transpired anyway. In any case, largely as a consequence of IRCA, on March 20, 1998, the Mexican Congress approved a momentous constitutional amendment that allowed dual nationality, finally harmonizing law and reality in a country where the two rarely match. Mexico concluded that the best way to defend the rights and interests of its citizens in the United States . . . was for them to become U.S. citizens. This decision, a result of the partial transformation of the country's attitudes toward migrants, logically enough further modified them. The amnestied migrants remained Mexican, though they had become American; from traitors, they had moved to being what the next Mexican president, Vicente Fox, would call them, as soon as he was elected: heroes. He was not alone in this; the president of the Philippines, Gloria Macapagal-Arroyo, calls her country's emigrants "modern heroes."

Indeed, Mexicans' opinions about migrants were changing, much for the better. In a 2004 poll taken in both countries, 63 percent of Mexicans thought migrants in the United States learned English, while only 42 percent of Americans thought so; 65 percent of Mexicans thought migrants were law-abiding, while only 51 percent of Americans thought so; and 94 percent of all Mexicans thought their compatriots in the United States worked hard. This shift translated into official views and government policies. Zedillo was the first Mexican chief of state to visit Mexican communities in California without first stopping in Washington or New York on the same trip; he set the stage for what would take place under his successor, the first Mexican president from a sending state since Cárdenas in 1934. Manuel Avila Camacho (1940–46) and Gustavo Díaz Ordáz (1964–70) were both born in Puebla, but in their era the majority of the state's dwellers had not yet moved to Manhattan. Fox came from Guanajuato, perhaps the epitome of a sending state for more than a century. Just as important, Fox was of immigrant stock himself: on his mother's side, his grandfather came to Mexico from Asturias, in Spain; his paternal grandfather emigrated from Germany to Cincinnati, and his son then went on to Mexico. He considers himself a descendant of immigrants, the only president of Mexico in modern times to have that recent history, and to believe in it, beyond symbolic visits to ancestors' hometowns in Spain.

Not surprisingly then, Vicente Fox put Mexican migrants at the top of his agenda with the United States, as we shall see later, and by so doing broke with traditional Mexican foreign policy stances in regard to Washington. The sea change he introduced in the country's approach derived from a simple fact: Fox was just taking note of changes that had already occurred on the ground, and consequently adjusting foreign policy to those changes. He was adapting policy to shifts in attitudes toward the migrants, in their origins and destinations, in their numbers and social profiles, and also to a major modification of the Mexican business community's approach to the issue of migration, as illustrated by the paradox of Mexicana Flight 001. These adjustments in Mexican business practices, which reflected the growing numbers and purchasing power of Mexicans north of the Rio Grande, were especially important to a president who had been elected with the support of the business community, and who boasted constantly of belonging to it (in fact, Fox had been a remarkable Coca-Cola marketing executive, but a mediocre businessman on his own).

Many Mexican companies had become huge multinational behemoths. They also realized the obvious: if their customers moved north, they should too, and they did. Televisa (the largest Spanish-language television network in the world) was among the first to do so. As early as 1961, it set up shop in the United States, founding the Spanish International Network, bought by Hallmark in the 1980s and renamed Univision. In 1992 Televisa, together with Venevision from Venezuela, repurchased 25 percent of Univision and signed a long-term contract with it, providing Univision with endless hours of Mexican-produced programming. Quickly, Univision became the fifth largest television network in the United States, and in 2006 tried, in vain, to purchase all of Univision, betting on a continued expansion of the Hispanic market. Even without immigration reform, according to its anchors, the Univision nightly news outranks CBS and ties NBC most nights in New York, Los Angeles, and Miami.

Another case is Grupo Maseca, the world's largest producer of tortillas. It initiated operations in the United States, through Gruma Corporation, in 1977, acquiring small tortilla factories still operating traditionally at the time. Today its products are sold in more than 30,000 outlets throughout the United States; total tortilla sales in the United States amount to roughly $1.9 billion yearly, and Gruma controls approximately a third of that market. It owns tortilla plants in Texas, Indiana, Kentucky, and California; Gruma Corporation's sales in the United States represent 53 percent of Maseca's sales worldwide; the domestic Mexican market only accounts for 28 percent of its global sales. It is not rocket science to understand that its first customers were recently arrived Mexicans, then Central Americans with a maize culture (although Maseca makes both corn and wheat tortillas), who continue to prefer traditional Mexican food to its Americanized alternatives, and finally Mexican Americans. But perhaps the most interesting aspect of Gruma's evolution is that in late 2006 it began advertising in English on television in San Antonio, and plans to do so on national networks as of 2007. It wants to appeal to unhyphenated Americans, who are now eating tortillas at McDonalds, Kentucky Fried Chicken, Taco Bell, Chili's, Chipotle, etc. Why not? After all, tomato salsa has surpassed ketchup as the main source of processed tomato food products in the United States.

Bimbo is a further example, holding a virtual monopoly on packaged bread and pastry products in Mexico. It entered the American market in 1984, founding Bimbo Bakeries (perhaps not the wisest choice of names, given the deeply Catholic and conservative character of the Servitje family, who created and owns Bimbo in Mexico). Bimbo Bakeries produces, distributes, and sells bread, tortillas, Mexican junk food, and pastries, almost entirely for the Hispanic market. It owns fourteen plants in the United States, located in California, Colorado, Oregon, and Texas, having recently acquired other companies in the United States, including Mrs. Baird's, Four-S, and, in 2002, Oroweat and Entenmann's on the West Coast. Today, American sales represent 26 percent of Bimbo's total business (including activities in Mexico, Central America, Argentina, and Brazil). Along with countless other, much smaller firms, these Mexican corporate giants began to invest, manufacture, and sell their wares in the United States—not a new, complex, adverse environment for their sales, but indeed, rather well-traveled territory. They knew how to sell bread, tortillas, soap operas, and CDs to Mexican consumers: that's exactly what they had always done; now they just cater to the same consumers who have simply relocated to the United States. Granted, previously they operated only under highly protected monopoly conditions in Mexico, but that was also—and remains—largely the case in the United States. Who else other than Televisa can produce sufficient telenovelas to fill Univision's airtime? Who else can deliver the same tortillas as back home, at a similar price and in similar packaging, to Mexicans in Oregon, Raleigh-Durham, or Philadelphia? Like all successful companies with powerful marketing divisions, they know the importance of accommodating their customers' tastes, whims, and needs. They do, and so do other companies—like Mexicana de Aviación. When it decided to modify its schedule, the airline was simply doing what many others were: listening to its customers, and adapting to their demands. The interesting aspect of the affair lies in who the customers are, and want they want.

TWO

The trends briefly described above were not all purely felicitous, however. Calling migrants heroes, or no longer treating them as Mexicans who lost their bearings and betrayed their country, can lead to a more balanced and cautious approach regarding why people leave, and what it means for a country like Mexico to have lived now for more than a century with a significant share of its population residing abroad. But it can also lead to a bitter, divisive, highly politicized debate about the origins and responsibility for out-migration. This is exactly what happened as Mexico's political system became, at long last, more democratic. As the issue acquired greater national traction—because of its broader reach and impact—it also became much more politicized. As this occurred and as rotation in power and free and fair elections became the norm in Mexico—at least at a federal level—a blame game emerged. Candidates for national and regional office began attributing the responsibility for emigration, and the underlying causes that generate it, on the Other: their rivals, adversaries, and enemies. In the 2000 election, candidate Vicente Fox blamed the PRI's seventy-year authoritarian rule for out-migration; in the 2006 presidential vote, the two opposition candidates, predictably enough, blamed Fox. They all tended to agree that having one of every ten Mexicans living in the United States was a painful reflection of Mexico's failure as a nation; that recent economic policy—indeed, any economic policy—had not worked; and that the solution to the shame and tragedy of nearly 400,000 departures every year—and one death daily at the border—was to create jobs and fix things at home. All of which was partly true, but begged the question of why, for over a century, Mexico had not been able to come to grips with the issue and put its house in order.

This "failed nation" perspective dovetailed neatly in the early years of the twenty-first century with its American corollary. Instead of shipping people north, Mexico should, according to conservative U.S. critics, "get its act together." Colloquial euphemisms aside, this generally reduces the complex migration phenomenon to a few worn, inaccurate bromides: Mexicans should "stop having babies" (in fact, Mexican population growth today is very low, and the population is rapidly aging); Mexico should "fix its economy and create jobs" (in fact, Mexico has now enjoyed almost twelve years of modest but sustained economic expansion for the first time in forty years, but, even when it does grow, migration does too); the solution lies in "eliminating corruption and becoming democratic" (in fact, Mexico is now a representative democracy, as much as any Latin American nation, and if corruption were the issue, Brazil and Argentina would probably be Latin America's largest sending countries, instead of the opposite). Some of these same critics subsequently simplify matters even further, engaging on occasion in racist, ignorant, or downright nonsensical approaches. A few sometimes give the impression they believe immigration from Mexico is a recent phenomenon; others suggest that only countries with serious domestic problems generate migration, i.e., that there is only a "push" factor, not a "pull" one. But if that were the case, then every nation from which millions of immigrants left across the globe and across three centuries would be "problem countries," from England and Germany to Japan, China, Korea, and India, without forgetting Spain, Italy, and Jewish communities all over the world. It is worth recalling that, after all, between 1846 and 1932, 52 million *European* immigrants left their homes for good, mostly to the United States. Despite their simplistic nature, these notions reinforce the Mexican view of out-migration as a symptom of failure; successful nations do not have so many of their citizens seek work abroad; if jobs are not available at home, there is something fundamentally flawed about the national character, origin, or destiny.

Both views—the Mexican one, which places the blame in general on the powers that be and in particular on the people in office, and the American one, which points at some deeper dysfunction—are false. Serious scholars in the two countries, as well as in Europe, have pinpointed the multiple causes that generate emigration all over the world, and especially from Mexico to the United States. According to legend, it all began many years ago, in 1894, when executives from the Gary, Indiana, Pullman railroad-car plant sought to break a strike by bringing in Mexican scabs from Chihuahua. In fact, like most legends, this one is probably inaccurate: migration began earlier, with the construction of railroads over the last two decades of the nineteenth century from Mexico City to the border and on into the U.S. Midwest. The *enganchadores* (or contractors, in a poor translation; the British Navy term "press-gang" might render the gist of the expression more faithfully) began coming to Mexico as early as 1870 to hire—some would say enslave—Mexican laborers to build the railroads or toil in other occupations to the

North. As broader ties were established between U.S. business and the Porfirio Díaz regime in Mexico, more and more of them were invited—or enticed—to work north of the border. The railroads were crucial for the process: the enganchador (a Mexican) would receive a request from a U.S. contractor; he would pay the Mexican military or police to "arrest" ("kidnap" would be a better word) a group of potential laborers, who would then be tied up with rope (which is why the process was known as "*la cuerda*") and placed on the next northbound train. To build our railroads, by the way, we in Mexico also imported manpower from China, with similar, if not worse, mistreatment.

Over the next one hundred and some odd years, out-migration from Mexico to the United States continued, only temporarily ceasing (and not entirely) during the Depression, which coincided with a period of significant land redistribution in Mexico. Before and during World War I, despite an end to immigration from Europe and Asia to the United States, it persisted. After a brief period of deportations and restrictions, it picked up again in the 1920s, slowed down in the 1930s, and then literally exploded, most notably during World War II. Dramatic labor scarcities in the United States as a result of the war effort led to the establishment, in 1942, of the Bracero Agreement, which essentially legalized unlimited immigration from Mexico, with the full cooperation of both governments, and paved the way for more than 4 million Mexicans coming to the United States until the program was terminated in 1964. Its suspension, though, did not deter migration; it just made it illegal, but tolerated. During the following twenty years, another 5 million Mexicans traveled to the United States, though a large percentage returned home, so the net inflow was much smaller: around 2 million. These were illegal, unauthorized, or undocumented, in the strict sense of the word, depending on the political correctness and connotations of the terminology one wanted to use. But they were completely accepted by the U.S. and Mexican governments, both of whom enjoyed the best of both worlds: a de facto situation that met their interests, and a de jure situation that made everything tolerable for everybody.

After 1986, and the Immigration Reform and Control Act (IRCA), often referred to in Mexico as the Simpson-Rodino Law, emigration continued at roughly the same rate, except that part of it was now legalized, through the act's amnesty provisions and subsequent family reunification consequences, and part remained unauthorized, though, once again, tolerated. What was known as the infamous Texas Proviso, legislated by the Texan congressional delegation in the 1950s, and which exempted employers from any sanction for employing "illegal aliens," was eliminated, and replaced by purported "employer sanctions." Except that employers were not asked to verify the authenticity of the documents (Social Security number, green card) they were obliged to request. The loophole in IRCA's "employer sanctions" derived from the absence of any stated obligation for employers to preserve verifiably authentic copies of these documents. So, predictably enough, very soon after 1986, an entire cottage industry of forged documents sprang up across the United States. I was able, for a pittance, to purchase a fake Social Security card and a false Permanent Resident ID (green card), and to publish copies of both in separate articles in *Newsweek* and the *Los Angeles Times* in 1990—evidence of just how obvious all of this was to everybody involved. Business as usual continued until the mid-1990s, when quantitative and qualitative changes unleashed a significant transformation of the status quo. A number of factors brought about a dramatic sharpening of the effects of out-migration, which in turn provoked a reaction in the United States from 1996 onward, thus generating a crisis in relations between the two nations from the late 1990s until today.

Those factors were largely foreseeable. One was the succession of economic crises in Mexico: 1976, 1982, 1987–88, 1994–95. By the time of the last one, patience on the part of myriad Mexicans had grown thin; they were increasingly inclined to leave, and did. Another was that, simultaneously, the United States was experiencing its longest, though not necessarily strongest, period of economic expansion—with a particular demand for low-cost, low-skill labor—since World War II. And third, NAFTA—the North American Free Trade Agreement signed by Canada, the United States, and Mexico, which came into effect on January 1, 1994—exacerbated both factors, though it did not create them. The trade opening or liberalization under way in Mexico since 1985 had already begun to de-structure the Mexican countryside, which, despite emigration and urbanization, remained overpopulated in relation to agriculture's contribution to the gross domestic product (GDP). Farm subsidies of all sorts—a stalwart of Mexican economic policy since the 1930s—were cut back starting in the late 1980s. As Mexican farms began to change—some becoming modern and highly competitive, others falling increasingly behind the rest of the world in corn and bean yields, for example—the numbers started evening out: fewer and fewer people worked in the countryside, and agriculture's share of GDP also declined. NAFTA just intensified this trend.

It probably accelerated the rate of displacement of people off the land and from previously protected or subsidized jobs in Mexico, but it is extremely difficult to calculate whether significantly fewer displacements would have occurred in its absence.

The economic structural reforms of which NAFTA was simply the crown jewel had begun a decade before in Mexico, and were starting to take effect roughly at the time NAFTA became the law of the land. Moreover, some of its features, particularly as regards the rural areas, were postponed until 2008, when full liberalization will take place in corn, bean, and powdered milk imports. With average corn yields in Mexico on nonirrigated land at less than 1.5 tons per hectare, compared to between 7 and 8 in Iowa, Kansas, and Nebraska, and over 10 in Central Europe, it is quite likely that droves of corn cultivators will be driven off the land in 2008. It is unclear, though, whether the rest of Mexican society should continue to subsidize 2.5 million families that will never escape from poverty growing corn on barren, rain-fed, tiny plots of land.

But as NAFTA immensely facilitated the exchange of goods across the border, it also encouraged the flow of people, though that was not its purpose. As the twentieth century came to a close, then, the accumulated magnitude of Mexican emigration—i.e., the stock, though not necessarily the flow—and its impact on Mexico and in the United States, rose exponentially. Perhaps most critically, as on so many occasions in immigration matters, the unforeseen consequences of certain policies changed the perception and the reality of the Mexican presence in the United States. As pressure built up on the Clinton administration to "do something to control our borders," it implemented a series of reforms that, in sum, broke the traditional process of circularity. Since the very beginning, Mexicans, like emigrants from all over the world, came and went; the Italians did the same thing in Argentina and the state of São Paulo in Brazil for a while; the Japanese did it in the United States and Brazil. Farm workers would go up for the harvest, move north with the weather and the fall, and return to Mexico during the winter. This is what traditionally explained the apparent paradox behind the numbers: far more Mexicans crossed into the United States than those who were counted as being there at any one time, and immense numbers were deported, conveying the sense that many more "made it." But as we shall see below, the minute it became more dangerous, more expensive, and more difficult to come and go, the circular motion was arrested and people stopped going home. What's more, they began to call on their families to accompany them. So a similar number of Mexicans as before were leaving the country, but now they were staying in the United States, reaching perhaps a critical mass or "tipping point" that generated the impression that the United States was literally being swamped by a wave of Latinos from Guanajuato.

The key point of this schematic and excessively brief summary is to illustrate how there have been both a constant and a trade-off in migration from south to north ever since it began. With nuances that do not alter the essence of this analysis, as we saw in the previous chapter, the yearly, overall total of Mexican out-migration to the United States, since just before World War I, has been relatively stable over time even in absolute terms, let alone as a percentage of the population of Mexico. What has varied enormously over different periods during the century involved is the share of legal and illegal, authorized or unauthorized migration, and more recently, whether they come and go or stay in the United States (the circularity phenomenon). There have been times when everything was neither legal nor illegal: the distinction simply did not exist. There have been times when almost all immigration was legal, as occasionally during the Bracero era, excepting of course the massive deportation period in 1953–54 known as Operation Wetback. There have been times when everything was illegal, but consciously tolerated, as during the "voluntary deportation" stage (see below), from 1964 to 1986.

Douglas Massey from Princeton University generously shared with me his evaluation of this process. He used official data to compute the rate of migration to the United States through various categories, measuring the flows per thousand Mexicans, tabulating legal immigration through the number of new permanent resident aliens admitted into the United States each year; measuring temporary legal workers by the number of Mexicans entering each year on temporary visas (braceros in the past, H2 workers today). Illegal migrants, of course, cannot be measured so straightforwardly, so Massey uses two indirect but acceptable indicators for this purpose: apprehensions for the number of Mexicans arrested while attempting an unauthorized crossing of the border, and deportations of Mexicans arrested within the American interior. According to Massey, we cannot make strong or exact statements about exactly how constant the total inflow might be. Nonetheless, over the past century, there is clearly a general relationship between the volume of entries through different channels—legal and unauthorized.

Before 1907 the entry of Mexicans in any category was tiny. However, with the conclusion of the so-called Gentlemen's Agreement with Japan in 1907, restricting Japanese migration, U.S. employers in the West began seriously to recruit Mexican workers. Since there were no restrictions on Mexicans at this point, they came in as legal immigrants. Once World War I broke out, the U.S. government began to assist employers by setting up federal labor recruitment programs, and after the United States entered the war in 1917 recruitment of Mexicans grew significantly. The end of the war brought about a dip in legal immigration, but once the United States passed discriminatory quotas to prevent the entry of southern and eastern Europeans in 1921, American employers once again looked southward. Mexican immigration experienced an unprecedented surge that occurred in two waves, 1923–24 and 1926–27. Rates of legal migration to the United States during the 1920s exceeded those observed at any point thereafter, with the exception of the massive legalization authorized by IRCA in the late 1980s and early 1990s. Aside from that unique episode, the rate of legal migration has never come close to rates observed in the 1920s. So, during a few years in that decade, *approximately 10 percent of the entire Mexican-born population resided in the United States: almost exactly the same proportion that exists today,* as sociologist Jorge Durand kindly pointed out to me.

After the stock market crash of 1929 and the onset of the Great Depression, of course, the United States reversed course and undertook massive deportation campaigns to round up and expel hundreds of thousands of Mexican workers. On a theoretical graph tracking all these figures, the curve pertaining to the deportation rate is the mirror image of that of the legal immigration rate, delayed by about ten years. The deportations ended all movement from Mexico and rates in all categories fell to zero by the late 1930s, helped during the Cárdenas administration by the resumption of the Mexican Revolution's land reform program. With U.S. entry into World War II came the Bracero Program. The rate of Bracero migration once again surged during the war, but never equaled the peak rates of the 1920s. After the war, the program was scaled back and the rate of contract worker migration fell. But labor demand didn't, and U.S. employers began to recruit Mexican workers outside of the program as undocumented workers. From the late 1940s through the early 1950s, undocumented migration began to increase rapidly again. A recession at the end of the Korean War and the height of the McCarthy era combined to produce a wave of anti-immigrant hysteria which culminated in Operation Wetback in 1953–54. During this period the border was militarized and apprehensions surged from a rate of around eighteen per thousand to about twenty-seven per thousand. At the same time that the U.S. Congress authorized Operation Wetback, however, it also doubled the quotas of the Bracero Program and most of those deported as unauthorized migrants simply reentered the United States as braceros. The peak of bracero migration in the late 1950s corresponds to the nadir of undocumented migration.

In 1964 and 1965, two things happened. The Bracero Program ended and amendments to the U.S. Immigration and Nationality Act placed the first-ever numerical limitations on permanent legal immigration from Mexico, through an overall ceiling for the western hemisphere, although at the same time the Hart-Celler Immigration Act eliminated the admission system based on discriminatory nationality quotas that had restricted immigration from all over the world since the 1920s. So undocumented migration from Mexico rapidly increased, and in 1986 reached levels equal to those observed on the eve of Operation Wetback in 1951–52. Given the political sensitivities of the post–civil rights era, American authorities could not launch a massive deportation campaign as in the 1930s, or a massive militarization of the border as in the 1950s; consequently, Congress passed the Immigration Reform and Control Act instead. IRCA adopted a two-pronged approach—legalizing undocumented farm workers and long-term residents of the United States, while gradually expanding border enforcement. During IRCA's legalization period, extending from 1988 to 1992, the relative number of Mexicans admitted to permanent resident status surged to an all-time high, but then fell sharply back to historical levels. Legalization—i.e., IRCA's amnesty provisions—dramatically reduced undocumented migration over the same period, which dropped by about half, from a rate of twenty-one per thousand to eleven per thousand.

In 1994, the Clinton administration signed NAFTA into law, and simultaneously increased border enforcement, possibly to prevent the further integration of labor markets, or perhaps just coincidentally, but either way encouraging the integration of all other North American markets, a fundamental contradiction that was only exacerbated by subsequent events. Today, legal immigration and contract labor migration are growing modestly, and while deportations are climbing, apprehensions are falling. Most important, though, the increasing concentration of enforcement resources along the border has induced workers who used to circulate back and forth to hunker down in the north and send for their family members. As a result, deportations are rising, and the size of the undocumented population is rapidly increasing—not so much through an increase in undocumented entries, but as a consequence of a sharp decline in departures, and the ensuing, virtual end of circularity.

Indeed, the net permanent outflow from Mexico to the north remained remarkably steady over this very long period, rarely dipping much below 200,000 per year, infrequently surpassing 350,000 per year. To quote Massey and two of his colleagues: "Considering the entire historical panorama of Mexico-U.S. immigration, what has changed over time is not so much the fact or rate of immigration as the auspices under which it has occurred. From 1900 to 1929, Mexicans entered as legal immigrants, from 1942 to 1964, as seasonal workers, and from 1965 to 1985 as undocumented migrants. The rate of legal immigration during the 1920s was higher than at any time up to

1991, and the rate of undocumented migration (measured by the apprehension rate) during the early 1980s was roughly comparable to the rate of bracero migration in the late 1950s" (Douglas S. Massey, Jorge Durand, and Nolan J. Malone, *Beyond Smoke and Mirrors*). The impressive growth of the number of Mexicans in the United States since the early 1990s—which nonetheless has not surpassed historical highs *in relation to Mexico's population*—stems not so much from a quantitative expansion of the flow of migrants as their metamorphosis from seasonal migrants to permanent settlers, or immigrants. This in turn was a result of post-IRCA border enforcement and interior policies that did not deter migrants from going to the United States, but certainly did discourage them from going back to Mexico every year.

In this long historical process lies the reason why Mexicans in general see migration in a different light from Americans, even well-meaning ones, when the latter underline the imperative need for everybody "to play by the rules." What are the rules? Mexicans ask. Americans answer: the law, and everyone must respect it, and consequently wait patiently in line at the U.S. Embassy on Paseo de la Reforma in Mexico City, or at the nine general consulates or thirteen consular agencies in Mexico, to obtain a visa of one type or another. Except that the laws have changed countless times, and moreover, the "rules" have always been different from the "laws." So which is it? Today's law or yesterday's rules? The laws and rules applied to others, or those in force for Mexicans during more than a century and still going strong? The laws that have alternately authorized and prohibited immigration, or the rules that have always allowed and encouraged it? How do the Lou Dobbses of the world want young Mexicans, whose ancestors, over four or five generations, have been migrating in one fashion or another to the

United States, to understand and abide by what has largely been an American fiction, i.e., that the United States, being a nation of laws, has always dealt with this issue respecting the law?

One of the most symptomatic, though certainly not the most crucial, indicator of this disconnect resides in the terminological dispute. Americans, particularly of a conservative inclination, refer to foreigners without proper papers as "illegal aliens," underlining the qualifier. Mexicans, chiefly those of progressive political persuasions, systematically resort to the euphemistic notion of "undocumented workers," stressing that they are neither legal nor illegal but simply lack documents, and that they have a special role in the United States: they come to work. Liberals north of the border, and realists south of it, have attempted on occasion to bridge the gap by choosing the term "unauthorized workers," that seeks to incorporate both the fact that there is an issue of legality, but not *only* of legality. In other words, the status of these individuals is tolerated, or even encouraged, by both countries. Mexicans, mainly in the political arena, cannot live even with this elliptical recourse: in their politically correct view, the only issue at stake is the existence of a transnational labor market; legal status is at best secondary and, indeed, largely meaningless. This, schematically summarized, has always been Mexican immigration-studies pioneer Jorge Bustamante's view. He and his colleagues underline the fact, illustrated by innumerable anecdotes on the border, of the "don't ask, don't tell" approach to migration by the Border Patrol and Congress. These anecdotes include stories of Immigration and Naturalization Service (INS, now Immigration and Customs Enforcement, or ICE) agents playing soccer with migrants; of coyotes negotiating with border authorities the place and time of collective entry; of United States Attorney General designates missing their chance for glory because of undocumented or illegal Mexican nannies taking care of their children while they made their career; of the decade-old policy of so-called voluntary deportation, whereby, in exchange for waiving their right to a hearing before a judge after lengthy and costly detention, Mexican migrants apprehended by the Border Patrol were shipped back at the closest point of entry, with the full knowledge of their absolute determination to try again, frequently on the very same day. Which makes sense: every night spent at jump-off points on the Mexican side (Tijuana through the mid-1990s, Sasabe and Nogales in the early twenty-first century) is a double whammy; it costs money, and delays the moment when income begins and preliminary outlays end. Under these conditions, it is not surprising that Mexicans have difficulty in taking without some circumspection repeated U.S. professions of faith in the sacred inviolability of the law. When, in the early 1990s, California Senator Pete Wilson pushed for, and later achieved as governor, the legal entry of tens of thousands of agricultural workers into his state, and then, again as governor, tried to drive them out through Proposition 187 once his state started suffering from its downsizing of its aerospace industries, it simply confirmed these suspicions. The discussion regarding the proper words reflects the debate and dichotomies about the most faithful interpretation of reality, and where the truth on most of these issues actually lies.

Where it lies depends largely on which side of the border one stands, and the purpose of this exercise is to articulate the conventional—and basically consensual—Mexican view. Following Jeff Bridges in *The Big Lebowski*, most Mexicans believe that the law, like the Chinaman in the Cohen brothers' cult classic, "is not the issue." The two countries have constructed, over the years, a segmented but partly unified labor market. Whatever their laws say, Americans from all walks of life tolerate, encourage, and enjoy the benefits of low-wage, low-skill, and high-comfort-zone labor from Mexico. The latter contributes enormously to the U.S. economy without receiving any acknowledgment from Americans for this contribution. Mexicans hope that one day, the United States will, instead of hypocritically accepting this situation by looking the other way and crying crocodile tears about breaking the laws, face up to it and formalize it: adapt legality to reality, instead of the other way around.

Vicente Fox, Mexico's previous president, became known, not always fairly, for his verbal faux pas and total indifference to political correctness. One case in which he clearly put his two cowboy boots in his mouth was in late 2005, when in relation to the migration chapter in U.S.-Mexican relations, he declared that Mexicans "had jobs in the United States that not even blacks were willing to take." African Americans rightly denounced Fox, and some black leaders (Jesse Jackson, Al Sharpton) were promptly invited to Mexico City so Fox could make amends. The Mexican president was, of course, stating, in the most undiplomatic and even outrageous language conceivable, what Mexicans think, and what in fact even his U.S. colleague proclaimed repeatedly during the entire 2005 immigration debate: Mexicans carry out work in the United States that Americans cannot, do not, and want not to fulfill. For George W. Bush, this was intuition derived from his life and upbringing in West Texas; for Vicente Fox, it was an involuntary, unconscious, racist slip of the tongue; for Mexicans from every walk of life, it is an article of faith.

Stoop labor from Mexico tends gardens and harvests fruit and vegetables—oranges, tomatoes, sugar cane—that the United States should probably not be producing anyway (if one truly subscribes to theories of comparative advantage and the international division of labor). These activities nonetheless survive in many regions of the country thanks to $5-a-day wages that substitute for costly or impossible mechanization, or the salaries that growers would have to pay for Americans to do the job. Would they do those jobs, at a "living wage"? Perhaps, but in an increasingly "free-trade" world, the consequences would not just be more expensive Delano grapes, Oregon strawberries, Washington apples, or Watsonville artichokes, but these entire sectors of U.S. agriculture going out of business. They could not compete with Mexican strawberries or avocados, Chilean grapes, or Central American seasonal vegetables, at least not without protectionist barriers. The case can be made that non-tradable goods and services—restaurants, construction, or landscaping, which cannot go abroad—would certainly survive without illegal labor, although undoubtedly at a higher price to consumers, but tradable goods and services (those than can move around the world at will) would not. So when Mexicans in the United States or back home argue that without them, important swaths of the American economy could not endure, they have a point—not an absolute one, not a perennial one, but a point nonetheless.

That point is reinforced when one actually meets the migrants before they arrive, as I did during my three visits to the northern Sonora desert between 2003 and 2006. They are a harrowing, desperate group, bunched together on a scrub-hill outside Sasabe, overlooking an invisible line that functions as a border. Sasabe is the proverbial hole in the ground: dry, dusty, destitute, whose only claim to fame before becoming the jump-off point for hundreds of thousands of migrants, was that José Vasconcelos lived there as a border guard near the turn of the previous century. Vasconcelos was Mexico's revolutionary Minister of Education in the 1920s; then, among other things, he convinced Diego Rivera and José Clemente Orozco to paint the murals in the National Palace, the Ministry of Education, San Ildefonso, and Chapingo. The migrants ignore their illustrious predecessor; frightened, poor, confused, they only know that as dusk approaches, the toughest part of their exodus to the north will begin: trekking two to three days through the Arizona desert till they get to Tucson or Phoenix, or are picked up somewhere by the coyote's truck or station wagon and driven farther inland. There are many small groups of five to thirty migrants, scattered across the highlands, squatting in the very relative shade provided by bushes and "trees" that look like bushes, shielding themselves from the 100-degree heat in early June; it will be more than twenty degrees hotter later in the summer. Most are in their twenties; some are younger, from fifteen on; every now and then a veteran emerges from the pack, and speaks more frankly and knowledgeably about the imminent danger. There are few women, at least in the summer months, when Mexican human traffic through Sasabe falls off, from nearly 3,500 per day in the early months of 2006 to less than a thousand. Conversely, many Central Americans are easily distinguishable, despite their efforts to disguise themselves as peasants from Chiapas: short, dark, with a slight, almost imperceptible lilt in their Spanish, but apparently familiar with their presumed hometowns of Motozintla, San Cristobal, Venustiano Carranza, and other villages in Chiapas. They are going north to settle.

There were about 2.5 million Central American–born individuals in the United States in 2005—nearly 1 million Salvadoreans, 600,000 Guatemalans, almost 400,000 Hondurans, and about 300,000 Nicaraguans. Of these, approximately half, or 1.3 million, were unauthorized, and about as many were authorized permanent residents, or with so-called TPS (Temporary Protected Status). Many of them are refugees from the wars of the 1980s, who eventually legalized their status; others are victims of Central America's recurrent natural disasters. Many of those who keep traveling north are relatives of those who settled years ago; their trip's tribulations dwarf those of their Mexican colleagues, since they suffer mistreatment and exploitation in Mexico too, often much more severe than in the United States. They are even more wary than their Mexican companions; when possible, they all remain silent, and defer to the coyote or *pollero*, their guide across the desert, who is Mexican and speaks for them, protecting his wards from the risk of being sent back to Guatemala or Honduras if picked up by the Border Patrol or handed over to the Mexican authorities. There is a difference: a Mexican will be sent back home, that is, across the border, from where he can try again the following day; a Salvadoran will also be sent home, but thousands of miles away, never to return in all likelihood.

The pollero knows his stuff. As rates began to rise—up to $5,000 from southern Mexico or Central America to New York or Chicago, including transportation, though most of the migrants interviewed during the summer of 2006 mentioned a much lower figure, around $1,500—trail guides became professional, big-time smugglers. Sneaking people across the border and up north has become big business, almost as big as drugs. The pollero takes care of his clients, up to a point; if things get complicated he may abandon them in the desert, but not often. For excellent reasons: smuggling is COD; payment is not effected until the migrant reaches his destination and his family, who foots the bills, or actually extends the newly arrived immigrant a loan he will repay with his initial wages. The *pollo* (the migrant) himself carries no money; and the risk of being caught the first or second time across is high enough to insure that full payment is the equivalent of a success fee. No successful crossing, no payment: those are the rules of the game.

These migrants' educational level is abysmally low: elementary school at best in most cases, and only rarely high school. They still come largely from rural areas, either the countryside itself, or what Mexicans often refer to as the paved-over country: small towns that demographically qualify as urban, but in fact remain culturally and socially agricultural. The percentage stubbornly remains at between 60 and 65 percent rural and 35 to 40 percent urban. Their reasons for leaving are obvious: they can't make ends meet, prices for the goods they grow on their meager parcels of land are depressed and no longer subsidized, and they have a cousin or a brother or a friend up north who has made good. In many cases, their ancestors began this rite of passage nearly a century ago. Most barely receive the minimum wage ($12 a day in most of Mexico) or its equivalent, and hope to make upwards of $6 or $7 an hour in the United States on entry into the labor market, often with as much as sixty hours of work a week. Later, they can move up to $10 or $12 an hour. They intend to go just about everywhere: one migrant, at fifteen still too young to shave, said he was going to Kentucky to work in the tobacco fields; either he knew his geography well, or his smuggler had coached him splendidly.

The pollos were mostly bunched together in Altar, a slightly more hospitable place than Sasabe, about fifty miles south of the line, where the smugglers stuff people into pickup trucks and minivans. There the pollos buy their backpacks—there are dozens of street stands selling them at a migrant Wal-Mart, as one clever U.S. reporter called the shops (Charles Bowden, "Exodus: Border-Crossers Forge a New America: Coyotes, Pollos and the Promised Van," *Mother Jones*, September/October 2006)—along with water and the other basic necessities for the upcoming trip. The migrants know the trek will be dangerous, and that some may die if they do not stick together. They also know they are likely to get caught a couple of times before succeeding, and that they will be deported only across the border to Nogales, a hundred or so miles east, if they can prove or persuade their captors of their Mexican origins (Central Americans, if detected, are, as stated above, sent back to their home countries). And most of all, they know they have to keep trying until they get across, for a very simple reason. They have burned their bridges back home, sinking their pitiful savings and wretched belongings into the cost of the voyage, the smuggler's fee, and a few dollars to survive until they obtain employment at their final destination. Mexican consular officials from Nogales (on the U.S. side) tell the story of a pregnant woman in her late thirties, found in the desert with her feet horribly swollen and blistered by dehydration and too much walking, being tended to with exquisite care by a Border Patrol medic, steadfastly refusing the agents' entreaties to allow them to send her home to Oaxaca. According to U.S.-Mexican agreements, undocumented aliens intercepted by the Border Patrol can be deported by plane back to their homes, deep in the Mexican hinterland, on the condition they voluntarily accept the trip, in the presence of Mexican officials. Despite their pleas, the woman refused, simply explaining that she had nothing and nowhere to go back to and preferred to risk her life one more time. She was never heard from again.

The intentions of those poised to cross the desert are contradictory, on occasion insightful and identical to those of millions of their predecessors from all across the world over the past century and a half, on occasion confused and surprisingly naive. Some of them—the rookies—are thinking of just spending a couple of years abroad, and then returning home with the money they would salt away; actually, even before circularity ended in the mid-1990s, this rarely occurred and will almost certainly not happen now. Others, the veterans, cross only for a harvest or two: melon and watermelon in Arizona over the summer, then back to Mexico. They can afford this, since they know the ropes and are able and willing to travel without a coyote, saving a great deal of money. And then there are the majority, those who don't really know exactly what their intentions are, beyond the hope of progress. They want to send money to their families, generally overestimating the size of their actual remittances; they don't really want to become American citizens; they don't really want to return to Mexico (particularly those who have not yet formed a family); they want, as one said, their version of the American dream: "A car, a house, and a cute girlfriend."

THREE

Why do so many Mexicans take all of these horrible risks know-ingly? Why do they suffer excruciating pain, exhaustion, fear, and humiliation to make it to the other side? Why have they been doing this, in one way or another, for more than a century? Needless to say, the reasons are not only multiple, but not com-mon to all, at all times. Sociologists have studied migration in general, and the exodus from Mexico to the United States in particular, for decades, and have many good answers. But on a more individual scale, it is worth simply restating some of the conclusions the migrants all seem to reach and share.

The danger, to begin with, is relative, both on an aggregate level, and as perceived by each *paisano* ready to start the march across the desert. Over the past ten years, since the Clinton era–built fences began pushing immigration farther east from California to Arizona, approximately one migrant has perished every day; on average, today, more than 1,500 succeed daily. The chances of surviving, then, are quite high, even if just one death is intolerable and, in fact, easily avoidable. But most im-portant, everyone who leaves knows someone who left before. According to some polls in Mexico, more than 40 percent of all

Mexicans have family in the United States and over 60 percent know someone "abroad" (a euphemism: other than approximately 15,000 temporary or seasonal workers who travel to Canada every year, abroad for Mexico in this context is the United States). In a recent survey among Mexicans in Chicago, one of the oldest Mexican communities in the United States, half of those who responded said that the presence of family in Chicago was the main reason they had come there. That fact, plus a hundred years of emigration, plus a 2,000-mile border, plus the pot of gold at the end of the American Rainbow, explains one of the statistics that most terrifies U.S. conservatives and Americans of all persuasions. A May 2005 Pew Hispanic Center poll taken among Mexicans in Mexico showed that 46 percent of those questioned said that "if they had the means and opportunity to go to live in the United States," they would do so; 21 percent said they would do so even without authorization. The percentage is higher among men than among women, among those below thirty years of age than among those older than fifty, but, remarkably, is highest among those with a middle school (55 percent) or high school (49 percent) education. And, most surprising, the desire or propensity to emigrate is almost identical among the very poor (who earn up to three times the minimum wage, which in Mexico amounts to about $150 per month), the poor (who earn from three to seven times the minimum wage), and among the emerging middle class (who earn seven times the minimum wage). In other words, roughly half of all Mexicans, regardless of their income, age (except for the elderly), or education, would go north, if they could. What is perhaps most interesting, of course, is that they don't. Most estimates of yearly departures rarely go beyond 400,000, that is, less than a third of the annual new entries into the labor market, or less than one in one hundred of those Mexicans who are roughly the age of potential departure—fifteen to forty-five years of age.

At the end of the day, Mexicans emigrate for reasons similar to those of others throughout history. They are looking for better-paying jobs than the ones they can find and keep at home; they are not necessarily unemployed, and, in fact, generally are employed in the case of those who come from the cities—a growing segment. Most emigrants hold jobs—without some income they could not pay for the voyage—but low-paying ones. As long as the wage differential (up to ten to one) between the two countries remains as large as it is, and compensates in the mind of the migrants for the danger, fear, and misery of the exodus, they will continue to travel. This is why there is a basic contradiction in the viewpoint many people in the United States—liberals and conservatives—have of the process. If they want free trade between Mexico and the United States to work, capital must flow to Mexico to take advantage of lower wages to make American firms more competitive; but if wages are low enough to attract capital, they are also low enough to drive emigration. In fact, today, Mexico may be living the worst of both worlds: its wages are rising, and becoming less and less competitive in relation to China, India, or Vietnam, for example; but as low-skill wages in the United States also rise, however slightly, it still makes good business sense to emigrate. Particularly if—and this is just as weighty a factor—the new migrant's family has been going north for generations; if there is a sister community from his town or *ejido* somewhere in the United States; if he has family currently in the north; and if the going in Mexico is generally tougher than before.

On the other hand, Mexico has always had, but now more than ever, one of the best of all possible worlds in immigration matters. No matter how happy this might make the Samuel P.

Huntingtons of the world—who, despite his sophistication and intelligence, in his book *Who Are We? The Challenges to America's National Identity*, simplifies obvious truths such as that the assimilation of Mexicans into the U.S. melting pot is very different from other previous migrant currents—the fact is that Mexicans in the United States can live a good chunk of their existence as though in Mexico. One of the best examples is Chicago, which is possibly the oldest Mexican community in the United States and continues to receive perhaps the highest number of newly arrived Mexicans in the country. The Mexican consulate in Chicago is, among the forty-seven offices we in Mexico have in the United States, the one which still delivers (as of late 2006) the highest number of high-security consular IDs, more than three hundred per day. Although the only really Mexican soccer team north of the border is Jorge Vergara's Los Angeles Chivas, in Chicago, games of the Mexican national team at Soldiers' Field, despite tickets costing more than $30 a seat, are full: tens of thousands of migrants attend, all dressed in green "official" shirts costing more than $50 apiece. The television coverage in 2006 of Mexico's World Cup match against Angola achieved the highest national rating on that day, regardless of language; more, for example, than NBC's broadcasts of the U.S. Open golf tournament and the Chicago Cubs vs. Detroit Tigers baseball game combined.

Mexicans in Chicago eat Mexican, to the tune of $2.5 million a day in Mexican perishables, from avocados to nopales. They shop Mexican: La Garra, as the Mexicans from Chicago refer to it (Americans call it the Maxwell Street Flea Market), founded more than a century ago, sells everything: chiles from Zacatecas, Puebla, and Michoacán; spare parts (stolen and licit); tools; antiques; new and used clothes; shoes, sandals, or guaraches from León, Guanajuato; sombreros from Jalisco;

copper arts and crafts from Michocán; sarapes from Saltillol; blankets from Tlaxcala; and just about anything one can find on the streets in Tepito, where hundreds of thousands of Mexico City inhabitants congregate every weekend to purchase everything under the sun. Here, one can eat *tortas ahogadas* from Guadalajara, *atole* and *birria* from Jalisco, *tamales oaxaqueños* and even tacos from Mexico City (a rare species indeed). As Alberto Tinoco Guadarrama from Televisa puts it: "La Garra is a reflection of the 'Mexican way of life' . . . in the United States."

Every month, Chicagoans chew the fat for 10 million hours on the phone to Mexico; the Spanish-speaking radio audience in Chicago surpasses the million people mark, and stations like WOJO-FM and WLEY-FM have ratings higher than almost four share points: the highest for an English-language station is just over five. There are more than one hundred Mexican associations in the city. And needless to say, Mexicans in Chicago can watch Mexican television on Univision and Telemundo; they go out to Mexican movie theaters to watch Mexican films; they attend concerts by Ana Barbara and Los Broncos, by Los Tigres del Norte (who have a street named after them in Pilsen), by Luis Miguel, new groups like Belanova, and much older ones like Marco Antonio Solis (previously the lead singer of Los Bukis). *La Raza*, the most important Chicago publication in Spanish, has a weekly circulation of more than 190,000, twice that of the leading Mexico City weekly. When Huntington says that Mexicans do not learn English the way previous immigrant waves did, he is not only wrong or exaggerating—according to a George Mason University survey, only 7 percent of the children of Latino immigrants speak Spanish as a primary language and virtually none of their grandchildren do—but, most important, he neglects this factor. Granted, the low educational level of Mexican immigrants and the long hours they work (on occasion three shifts) make it extraordinarily difficult for the first generation to learn English. But the continuity and contiguity of Mexican immigration to the United States explains why Spanish works just fine, thank you, along with another unique feature of current immigration from Latin America. With the exception of a sprinkling of Haitians, Jamaicans, and Brazilians, every immigrant from the hemisphere speaks Spanish. Unlike the European or Asian waves of yesteryear, there is a common language to all. It makes an enormous difference. At a national level, 41 percent of Latinos think that immigrants do not have to speak English to be part of American society. According to a Pew Hispanic Center survey carried out in late 2002, almost 72 percent of foreign-born Hispanics (the overwhelming majority of which are Mexicans) predominantly speak Spanish. But conversely, 60 percent U.S.-born Latinos (largely second-generation) speak English proficiently. The problem, of course, is that Mexicans arrive younger than others before them, and their life expectancy is thankfully much longer.

All of these reasons explain why it was high time for Mexico to place immigration at the top of the U.S.-Mexican agenda in the year 2000, when Vicente Fox's election finally put an end to more than seventy years of virtual one-party rule in the country. There had been a previous window of opportunity, in 1992–93, when the NAFTA negotiations were under way. The official explanation (provided on many occasions by government officials themselves) of why the Mexican negotiators, under the stewardship of President Carlos Salinas de Gortari, did not insist on including immigration in the trade and investment talks was that if they did, their American counterparts would have demanded that energy, i.e., Mexican oil, also be placed on the table, and this last issue was simply nonnegotiable for Mexico. Even if he had wanted to, Salinas, according to this version, could never have convinced Mexicans to negotiate oil for people, so to speak. This last appreciation was confirmed by a poll taken years later, in 2004. When asked whether they would be in favor or against an agreement between Mexico and the United States in which the latter would give Mexicans more opportunities to work and live legally north of the border, and, in exchange, the former would give the United States greater access to its oil, gas, and electric power, 71 percent of Mexicans from all walks of life said they would oppose it, and only 18 percent said they were in favor; almost as noteworthy, public opinion among business and academic elites was 50 percent against and only 37 percent in favor. Undoubtedly these negative perceptions have much to do with the 2004 context: Iraq, George W. Bush, Minutemen on the Sonora-Arizona border, etc. Still, they are a reflection of what probably was a similar state of mind back in 1992.

Nonetheless, there are grounds for believing that the official story was nothing more than ex post facto justification for a decision made earlier. Mexico chose not to push for the inclusion of immigration because it would have certainly delayed the negotiations, possibly jeopardizing approval in the U.S. Congress. Salinas was in a hurry; he wanted to get NAFTA sealed, signed, and delivered before the 1992 U.S. presidential elections (he failed in this) and was totally uninterested in throwing a monkey wrench into the infinitely delicate machinery of trade talks and tariff negotiations. He was right in believing that immigration, with or without an energy quid pro quo, would have drawn out the process; what remains open to question, mainly in Mexico, but also in the United States, is whether a North American Free Trade Agreement without immigration, energy, infrastructure, and social cohesion clauses was better than no NAFTA at all. It is true, as George H.W. Bush was said to have exclaimed, that NAFTA with immigration or any taxpayers' dollars was dead in the water.

But another reason Mexican governments were not adamant about immigration until 2000 involved the traditional Mexican stance on the issue. In the final analysis, Mexico had always thought that it enjoyed the best of both worlds, and should not tinker with a status quo that could not truly be improved upon. According to this age-old perception, although the Mexican government continued to press for some sort of extension of the Bracero Agreement until the early 1970s, in most scholars' view its termination in 1964 was the best thing that could have happened to Mexico in a long time. According to conventional wisdom, the agreement encouraged corruption, mistreatment, swindling, and the devastation of many Mexican communities and families. Bribes were paid in order to obtain the legal permits; the lottery system never really worked; coyotes bought and sold slots in line, lottery numbers, or even visas; part of the withheld portions of the migrants' wages never reached their wallets; U.S. authorities abetted the exploitation of Mexican workers and did not enforce many of the provisions of their contracts regarding housing, transportation, salaries, and time off; all in all, it was seen as a terrible deal for Mexico. This had become an official history, which corresponded partly to reality, and partly to ideology, but it had established itself as the lore of the land.

Thus, at least since 1964, Mexico had on the one hand continued to enjoy the benefits of mass out-migration to the United States: safety valve considerations, remittances, social peace, regional redistribution of income, with no major disadvantages other than occasional incidents with United States, moderate discrimination against its nationals in the United States, and the broader challenges of emigration (the best and boldest are the ones who leave, communities and families are separated, Mexico foots the education and health bills, the United States enjoys its benefits, etc). On the other hand, it bore no responsibility for regulating the flow of migrants or cooperating with Washington on immigration, since the United States had always considered the matter a domestic one, which was really not Mexico's business. The country's authorities and experts always believed that their neighbor to the north would never be able to close down the border, and that any negotiation between the two countries on immigration would inevitably entail some sort of Mexican co-responsibility in deterring outflows of an unauthorized nature. Better let sleeping dogs lie.

Consequently, injecting immigration into NAFTA was a nonstarter for many reasons, and the opportunity was passed over. Moreover, one of the chief (over-) selling points for NAFTA during the 1993 debate in the U.S. Congress was that its approval would diminish illegal immigration from Mexico, and perhaps even eliminate it altogether, in time. It thus seemed contradictory to push for NAFTA as an antidote to immigration, and then include the issue in the same NAFTA negotiations. It goes without saying that those on both sides of the argument were equally mistaken: contrary to what its proponents argued, NAFTA did not deter, reduce, or eliminate immigration, legal or illegal, from Mexico. But unlike what its opponents maintained, it certainly did not create or significantly stimulate migration. At most, it might have contributed to a slight increase by expanding all sorts of exchange between the two countries, and by displacing some Mexicans from the land they used to work on, where they cultivated agricultural produce that was completely uncompetitive and doomed with the already consummated trade opening.

The NAFTA-immigration debate was a false debate, for the same reason that many of today's discussions in the United States on immigration are too: they simply ignore history. Extremists on the right are obviously wrong when they deride Mexico for "exporting people" today in order to increase remittances, forgetting that the process—immigration and remittances—is well over a century old; those who blame NAFTA for out-migration today, like many on the left in both Mexico and the United States, are also mistaken. Mass emigration from Mexico was around long before anyone even thought of NAFTA, before trade liberalization contributed to the displacement of peasants from the land in the 1980s, and even before industrialization in the 1940–80 period generated the same process. It will continue long after NAFTA has become totally assimilated by both countries' economies, and regardless of whether the last chapter of the trade opening—beans, corn, and powdered milk—takes place as scheduled in 2008, or is postponed.

Be it as it may, by the mid-1990s the entire migration context began to change. More than NAFTA, U.S. immigration reforms implemented from 1996 onward, sometimes as direct border enforcement policy, sometimes as welfare reform that affected the poor in general, and the Mexican, undocumented, immigrant poor specifically, transformed the issue's basic parameters. In particular, according to *The New Americans: A Guide to Immigration since 1965*, "In 1996 Congress passed welfare reform and immigration legislation partly in an effort to curtail unauthorized migration by limiting the public benefits available to noncitizen immigrants." Policies such as Operation Hold the Line or Gatekeeper, in El Paso and San Diego, respectively, that among other features included building a fence from the Pacific Ocean in Playas de Tijuana to beyond the local airport at Otay Mesa dozens of miles eastward, along with the hysteria on immigration in certain areas of the United States, all suggested that Mexico's "If it ain't broke, don't fix it" attitude was becoming unsustainable. Clearly, the Clinton administration's measures would not succeed in halting immigration. Nor was the United States ready for any kind of immigration deal that involved bilateral cooperation, but it was becoming equally evident that the old status quo—the best of both worlds, the ideal solution for Mexico—was disintegrating as the century came to a close. In addition, the traditional Mexican stance on all matters foreign—burying its head in the sand and rejecting any international responsibility—was also shifting, as a more democratic, mature, open and extroverted Mexico emerged on the international scene. As a binational panel quoted at length below concluded in the year 2000: "Essentially, until very recently, Mexico's policy on immigration had been to have no policy." This was no longer possible, even though it had not been totally true throughout the twentieth century. In fact, through the late 1920s, Mexico tried to dissuade emigration for nationalistic reasons; then it tried to neutralize deportations during the 1930s, and signed the Bracero Agreement in 1942, which required Mexican government cooperation, and finally threw in the towel on any policy in the early 1970s.

One of the most important factors contributing to a change in Mexican attitudes lay in the deadly consequences of the Clinton administration's policies. In April 1996, on Avenida del Oro and the corner of Capistrano, near the town of Temecula in the Santa Rosa Mountains southeast of San Diego, a van carrying twenty-five undocumented Mexican migrants overturned as it was trying to outrace the Border Patrol. Eight of the passengers died, seventeen were wounded, the driver was arrested and charged with smuggling, but some of the surviving passengers said the real pollero got away. The Mexican news media broadcast a local network video of the accident endlessly for several days, inflaming public opinion. The tragedy touched a raw nerve in Mexico, for many obvious reasons, but chiefly because such a degree of peril had never been apparent in more than a century of unauthorized crossings. Getting caught and deported, with or without a little roughing up, or a few racist comments by Border Patrol agents, was bad enough; dying in an overcrowded van in a ravine well north of the border was beyond the established limits. Unfortunately, this was an example of a much broader trend.

The fences or walls, enhanced Border Patrol surveillance, overreaction to strident scenes broadcast on U.S. television in the mid-1990s of Mexican immigrants swarming over the border and then bobbing and weaving through the traffic on the interstate highway from San Ysidro to San Diego, all converged to create an unwanted but not unexpected result. Instead of crossing roughly in the area comprised between the sea to the west and the Tijuana airport to the east, migrants were being squeezed inland, first into the mountains of eastern California, and subsequently, into the desert of western and central Arizona. Closing off the traditional crossing points did not deter immigration; nor did increasing the size of the Border Patrol along the southwest border, that approached nearly 9,000 agents in 2000, compared to 3,000 in 1990. By 2000 as many Mexicans and Central Americans as ever were streaming into the United States, though in relation to their own populations, the numbers remained roughly constant. But the dangers entailed by crossing through much more hostile and unknown terrain brought about two tragic, unforeseen consequences.

First, people began to die trying: by 1997, as we said, more than one Mexican was losing his life every day pursuing the American dream. By 2000, about five hundred people were dying per year, in largely avoidable tragedies involving dehydration, sunstroke, snakebite, and exposure. Second, as the risks and difficulties of crossing from Mexico to the United States without papers increased, the need for—and price of—polleros also rose. Instead of typically costing $200 or $300 to be guided across the border by the Mexican equivalent of Himalayan sherpas, or perhaps $500 to $700 to be taken all the way to Chicago, New York, or the Yakima Valley in Washington State, smugglers now began charging upwards of $1,000 to cross the mountains or the desert and up to $2,500 for safe passage to the Midwest or the Northeast. This, needless to say, totally altered the smuggling trade, from an almost artesanal, family business or cottage industry, into organized crime. Huge sums of money were to be made moving people northward from South and Central America, southern and central Mexico, to the tune of roughly $1,000 per head, and over a thousand daily crossings on average during the year.

Third, and perhaps more important, though less sadly, circularity came to an end. We already provided some numbers earlier on: apprehensions are declining (as fewer people are caught at the border, because fewer are coming and going); deportations are rising, because there are more Mexicans in the U.S. hinterland. But impressions are more important than statistics. As the price and the danger of crossing increased, and the opportunities of doing so without excessive stress diminished, without job availability undergoing an analogous reduction, Mexicans began, from 1996 onward, both to stay in the United States, instead of returning home for half the year, and to bring their families up with them, instead of leaving them back home and starting new families north of the border. As Mexicans began to spread out everywhere in the United States, they settled farther away from the border, and it became more difficult and costly to go home for holidays or whatever. As they gradually moved on from agricultural work to industry, services, etc., the seasonal nature of their employment gradually evolved toward permanence: they could keep their jobs all year, and they *had* to keep them all year in order to keep them at all. As suggested earlier, this is what explains the real increase in the numbers and dispersion of Mexicans across the land: they are settling. In Jorge Durand's felicitous formulation, Mexicans had been workers; they were becoming immigrants. Americans might want to think of what this means: do they prefer Mexicans to come and stay, or to come and go, or to have the best of both worlds: some settling down, and contributing to American life as they gradually become . . . Americans, and some commuting between the two countries, but remaining Mexican. They have the choice, but it is a choice. What is not reasonable—or feasible—is to reject Mexicans because they do not assimilate, and then make it more difficult, if not impossible for them to assimilate.

No one can assert that the Clinton administration—and its knowledgeable and decent INS team—was pursuing this sad state of affairs when it defined and implemented its new policies. The Clintonites did not seek to interrupt circularity and force people to stay in the United States instead of traveling home after their work for the year was done. Neither, of course, did they intend to kill Mexicans in the desert, nor invite organized crime into a new field of endeavor. But that is what happened, as almost always is the case with U.S. immigration policy: the name of the game has always been unintended and unforeseen consequences. Unfortunately but ultimately serendipitously for Mexico, these unexpected consequences of U.S. policy forced the country, for the first time, to approach migration from a different standpoint. One thing was to turn the other cheek to discrimination and exploitation of Mexican nationals in American fields or sweatshops; they had chosen to leave and were undoubtedly better off in Delano than in Zacatecas. Quite another was to dismiss or ignore the justified indignation of domestic public opinion over increasingly frequent tragedies in the desert, railroad cars, and flatbed trucks with hidden compartments, often involving women and children. One thing was to have a few altruistic but poorly trained and meagerly funded BETA Group officials—the Mexican equivalent of the Border Patrol—combating polleros on the southern and northern borders; quite another was to deal with organized crime shipping legions of people from south to north for huge sums of money, on occasion in collusion with the other, dreaded, sectors of organized crime: the drug cartels. Mexico's traditional stance was becoming untenable. Simultaneously, a window was opening in the United States for a different approach to the entire matter.

The window opened during the year 2000 for several reasons. The first was, as usual, strictly economic. Despite the brief turndown in the U.S. economy that year and the following one, the 1990s had witnessed the longest period of economic expansion since World War II. That alone had generated enormous demand for the low-skill, low-wage labor that Mexicans traditionally provided. So instead of Americans feeling that foreigners, with or without papers, were taking jobs away from them, they sensed that, on the contrary, they were permitting them to continue fueling an economic boom unlike any they had witnessed in nearly half a century. Some jobs, actually, were being taken away from Americans, by Mexicans (and others). But it did not seem to matter.

The meatpacking plants in Iowa are an excellent example. According to the U.S. Department of Labor's Bureau of Labor Statistics, there were nearly 520,000 people employed in the meatpacking industry in 2001. In the food industry as a whole, meatpacking and processing is the largest area of employment. In 2001 meat trimmers and cutters earned a mean annual salary of $17,960, and meatpackers and slaughterers earned a mean annual salary of $20,000: average wages in the slaughterhouses are thus half what they were in the 1960s, and many of the jobs were taken over by foreigners—mainly, but not only, Mexicans (Laotians and Central Americans fill part of the vacancies). In recent years the meatpacking industry underwent major changes in its structure and character. Large losses had occurred during the early 1980s, with more than thirty plants in the state shutting down. In the aftermath, several new industry leaders emerged, including companies like Tyson, ConAgra, and Cargill. These firms moved meatpacking plants away from urban areas, which were home to well-organized unions, to rural communities. Today, the top five beef companies (Tyson, Excel, Swift, Farmland, and Smithfield) control 89 percent of steer and heifer slaughter in the whole United States. As a result of its history (ever since the publication of Upton Sinclair's *The Jungle* and its impact on U.S. working conditions) and of this recent consolidation with its ensuing need to keep down expenses, the meatpacking industry has been a longtime opponent of workers' unions and pays well below the U.S. national average: the best way to keep *The Jungle* intact is through migrant labor. According to David Bacon in the *American Prospect*, "Today, Spanish is the language on the floor of almost every plant. Most workers come from Mexico, with smaller numbers from Central America. Employing recent immigrants has become standard practice."

The town of Storm Lake in northwestern Iowa is a perfect case study, as shown by an article published in the late 1990s in *Revolutionary Worker*. It has 10,000 inhabitants, a 2 percent unemployment rate, and just about everybody has a relative working either in Iowa Beef Processors (IBP), the second largest pork-packing plant in the world, or in a turkey-packing plant, Sara Lee's Bil-Mar. Three-quarters of the manufacturing jobs in the town are concentrated in these two plants. Originally, Storm Lake was settled by Swedes and Germans; now 1,500 Laotians and 600 Mexicans live there, including a small minority of Mennonites from Chihuahua. The Laotians are legal refugees, the Mexicans unauthorized workers. IBP began "hooking" Mexicans in the 1980s; by the 1990s tax exemptions and subsidies were provided to plants that set up shop there, which in turn drew in more migrants. A Mexican worker makes about $300 for a forty-eight-hour week, or $6 an hour. Altogether, the Mexican community in Storm Lake sends home around $5,000 a week in postal money orders. According to Mark Grey, an anthropologist at the University of Northern Iowa, the U.S. food-processing industry in the United States would go broke if it were not for immigrant labor.

Another case in point is Marshalltown, also in Iowa. Hiring Latinos solves a number of important problems for Marshalltown's meatpacking plant. First, the exodus of rural Anglo populations during the "farm crisis" in the 1980s did not reverse significantly during the 1990s. Indeed, Marshalltown's total population only grew between 1990 and 2000 because of the large influx of Latinos, from 25,178, of whom 248 (0.9 percent) were foreign-born, to 26,009 in 2000, of whom 3,265 (12.6 percent) were Mexican or Central American. Hiring these workers also helped the Marshalltown packing plant overcome a shortage of applicants during the thriving economy of the 1990s. Work in a meatpacking plant is simply not attractive to most Anglo workers. Even though wages rose during the 1990s, they are usually not high enough to attract local Anglos from other jobs. In 1997, for example, the average hourly wage in the Marshalltown plant rose from $7.50 to $9.55. In 2002, the average wage was about $10.50 per hour. For local Anglos, the wages are low relative to the difficult, dangerous, and distasteful nature of these jobs.

When asked in a survey about competition between immigrants and Iowans for jobs, 76 percent said immigrants "take jobs other Iowans don't want." For many Mexicans and Central Americans, meatpacking jobs are among the few industrial jobs for which they qualify, and the wages are high relative to those paid in the agricultural or service sectors where they also might find work. Mexicans, in a nutshell, are settling in Marshalltown; as two scholars who have studied the case in detail point out and from whose work this example is taken, "Mexican children are graduating from Marshalltown schools; they are fluent in English, have grown up in the United States and consider themselves American" (Mark A. Grey and Anne C. Woodrick in *New Destinations*). These trends are also taking hold elsewhere in the region: the Dakotas, Minnesota, Nebraska, Kansas, North Texas, and the Ozarks in Missouri. So much so that the federal government finally had to take steps to control the situation.

In December 2006, ICE agents raided six meat-processing plants owned by the Swift Corporation all over the country. The raids resulted in more than 1,200 allegedly undocumented immigrant workers being detained at the plants, many of who were hauled off by buses across state lines to be processed and later deported. The raid was trumpeted by ICE as a major victory in the "war on illegal immigration" and as the culmination of a successful investigation into an organized crime ring that was supplying fraudulent ID documents to these workers. The day after the Swift plant raids, ICE issued a press release announcing "that approximately 1,282 persons have been arrested as part of an ongoing worksite enforcement investigation into immigration violations and a massive identity theft scheme that has victimized large numbers of U.S. citizens and lawful U.S. residents." Of those, sixty-five had also been charged with criminal violations related to identity theft or other violations, such as reentry after deportation. ICE had just discovered what everyone knew: the U.S. meatpacking industry depended on low-skill, low-wage unauthorized labor, which was made possible by what George Bush called, in regard to the raids, "a system we have in place [that] has caused people to rely upon smugglers and forgers in order to do work Americans aren't doing. It is a system that, frankly, leads to inhuman treatment of people." Even the *New York Times* congratulated the president: "Mr. Bush showed yesterday that he gets it," it editorialized on December 21, 2006.

A booming economy provokes reactions to immigration—for the better—like nothing else; economic contraction produces similar results, but in the opposite direction. There is almost a perfect match between recessionary periods in American economic history and bouts of nativism in American attitudes toward immigration, between economic booms, and periods of openness and tolerance. The remarkable economic expansion of the 1990s generated a transformation of American views; the just-mentioned historical correlation led to one of the most important expressions of the window of opportunity cited above: Federal Reserve Chairman Alan Greenspan's testimony in Congress on February 27, 2000, in relation to declining American population growth and the fiscal, inflationary, and retirement consequences of the trend. He unequivocally proclaimed, "Immigration, if we choose to expand it, could also lessen the decline of labor force growth in the United States. As the influx of foreign workers that occurred in response to the tight labor markets of the 1990s demonstrated, U.S. immigration does respond to evolving economic conditions. But to fully offset the effects of the decline in fertility, immigration would have to be much larger than almost all current projections assume." This was no minor statement. A conservative, orthodox Central Banker was finally saying what everyone knew: immigration was good for the American economy, and the more voluminous the better. Clearly something was changing in American feelings toward immigration in general, and Mexicans in particular; the moment was ripe for seizing.

A second manifestation of the extraordinary shift in the weather took place on the other side of the political, ideological, and social spectrum. Traditionally, the American labor movement had been ambivalent about immigration. Made up largely of immigrants, it shared the generosity and bigheartedness of U.S. liberals on the issue, but also considered itself to be a victim of the entry of low-salary, low-skill, labor-rights-deprived undocumented workers from abroad. The conventional wisdom of the labor movement regarding undocumented immigration was that it drove wages down, or in any case kept them from rising, and made mincemeat of labor conquests achieved after long years of struggle. Right or wrong—and the technical case was easier to enunciate than to prove—this skepticism was deeply rooted in the leadership and rank-and-file of the American proletariat. Organized labor was especially opposed to guest-worker programs, and its malaise in regard to illegal immigration tended to spill over to opposition to immigration in general. Thus, it was surprising, to say the least, but extremely noteworthy, to see the AFL-CIO, at the February 2000 New Orleans yearly meeting of its executive council, adopt a totally new attitude toward immigration. It endorsed protection for immigrant workers and for a "new amnesty program . . . needed to provide permanent legal status for undocumented workers and their families," and encouraged the organization of newly arrived immigrants, in what after the fact seemed a perfectly logical adaptation to new times. The fastest growing sector of the American economy that could be organized was in the low-skill, low-wage sector of services generally provided by immigrants. Hotel workers, janitors, hospital nurses, restaurant workers, construction, and landscaping were the booming segments of the labor market, and they were significantly occupied by immigrants, legal or not. The unions, and particularly the AFL-CIO, had been losing the organizing battle since the 1970s, and what better way to unionize the unorganized than to legalize the illegal. This was the second fundamental factor in the window of opportunity.

A third element was what Vicente Fox and his team called the "Mexican democratic bonus," that is, the goodwill and trust that the advent of full-fledged electoral democracy and the eviction of the PRI from power would entail for Mexico in the United States and, indeed, all over the world. For years, on issues such as drug enforcement, border security, foreign policy, foreign investment, even trade, Mexico had suffered from being perceived—not always wrongly—as one of the last bulwarks of authoritarian rule in Latin America. One-party rule had begun to recede since the late 1980s, but the Revolutionary Institutional Party or PRI, retained a majority in Congress until 1997 and held on to the presidency until 2000. Fox and many Mexicans and Americans surmised, correctly as it turned out, that the end of the PRI era would give Mexico a certain premium or bonus on a number of negotiations and issues with the United States and the rest of the international community. This turned out to be true in the United Nations, where Mexico quickly conquered a nonpermanent seat on the Security Council, with full P.5 support (Mexico was the first country George Bush visited as president, while Fox was the Bush White House's first official guest), and on one major substantive question: the elimination of the hateful "drug enforcement certification" process, whereby the U.S. executive would "certify" or "decertify" countries each year in a message to the Congress, depending on how "well" these countries were cooperating with Washington on drugs. Although the suppression of this procedure benefited nearly every country in Latin America, it was largely at Mexico's urging that both the executive and legislative branches in Washington agreed to do so. After 9/11, though, and beyond the drug issue, the "democratic bonus" became very difficult to cash in on.

The last contributing factor to the window of opportunity was, paradoxically, the election of George W. Bush to the presidency of the United States. There is a long history of debates and disagreements among scholars in both countries regarding what type of American chief of state Mexico tends to get along better with. There have been good relations with both Democrats (Roosevelt, Kennedy, Clinton) and Republicans (Bush Sr., Gerald Ford), and bad relations with liberals (Carter) and conservatives (Nixon, Reagan). But it seemed clear that, as in the case of Ronald Reagan, another conservative Republican governor from a border state would be much more forthcoming on immigration than any alternative. It is worth recalling that the last "amnesty" granted to undocumented immigrants in the United States was signed in 1986 by none other than Ronald Reagan. For several reasons, it was logical to expect that George W. Bush would act similarly: familiarity with the issue firsthand; no enemies on his right willing and able to shoot down reform or agreements; a certain standing with the American people on the issue, given his credentials as a two-term governor of Texas. This assumption also seemed to be borne out by events during the first months of the Bush administration, as the latter quickly welcomed the Mexican proposal to begin talks on immigration, and also accepted the overall view of the agenda as put forth by the Mexican side.

FOUR

In this window of opportunity partly opened by his own election, Vicente Fox made things both easier and more difficult. From the very first days after his election in July 2000, for example, in a long interview with Sam Donaldson on ABC's *This Week*, the new Mexican president-elect began broaching subjects that were previously taboo in U.S.-Mexican relations. He referred to "open borders"—not "overnight," but soon. He spoke about "full mobility" of labor between the two neighbors; he talked about "freedom of movement" for people across the border, in the same way that there was, since NAFTA, a free movement of goods, tradable services, and capital. He painted a rosy picture of a hypothetical North American Economic Community, along European lines, associating Mexico with the United States and Canada, including comments that could have been interpreted as a call for a common currency for the three countries, and which provoked a strong backlash in official and media circles in Ottawa and Toronto during his Canada visit as president-elect in August 2000. He placed the immigration issue front and center on the bilateral agenda, often in undiplomatic or politically incorrect terms, but always forcefully, eloquently, and explicitly.

He did this for several reasons, some of them well-thought-out, others somewhat unconscious or naive, and others still quite disingenuous. Fox, coming from one of the main Mexican sending states, proud and sure of his "democratic bonus," was confident in his ability to convince Americans of just about anything. At the same time he was totally inexperienced in foreign affairs; to compound this conundrum, he had completely separated his foreign-policy team from his foreign-press team. Moreover, it took him quite a while to convince himself that he had actually won the election and become Mexico's first non-PRI president since the 1920s. Inevitably, he set off a strong reaction in the United States against his unabashed views. Yet he also forced many of his American interlocutors to address an issue they were never totally comfortable with, particularly while discussing it with Mexicans.

Many Americans were either dismayed or disconcerted by Fox's initial statements, expressed in the midst of the euphoria that enveloped the nation and his team in the days following the elections. They should have been understood for what they were: the spontaneous, extemporaneous, unscripted remarks by a man with no government or diplomatic experience whatsoever, made in the historic, heady context of unseating a one-party system that had ruled the country for seventy years. Those of us who did have a sense of their implications were not standing next to him when he took phone calls from abroad, or gave interviews to the U.S. media—only his wife-to-be and then spokeswoman, Martha Sahagún, as unprepared for victory as Fox was, and his personal assistant, Juan Hernández, a double-nationality Dallas resident from Guanajuato. None of the future members of his foreign-policy team, including myself, were able, during those hectic and glorious days, to dissuade him from what were not totally unreasonable grounds for those statements. He thought that by raising the bar as high as he did, he would achieve two goals: first, place the immigration issue at the center of the U.S.-Mexican agenda, which was a substantive decision he had already made; second, stake out his territory clearly, in order to begin the real and rhetorical negotiations from that level. And, in fact, he largely attained those twin objectives, though at a cost.

His declarations were subsequently tempered and diluted by more formal stances enunciated by the president-elect himself and his postelection transition team, particularly during a visit he made to New York, Washington, and Dallas in late August 2000, during which he met with, among others, President Clinton and presidential candidates Al Gore and George W. Bush. Fox established a distinction between his long-term vision— "open borders"—and his short-term goals—a better life for Mexicans in the United States. Once George W. Bush was finally declared the winner of the 2000 election, the two governments began to address the immigration issue realistically and constructively. Still, experts on both sides of the border, and former U.S. ambassador to Mexico Jeffrey Davidow, among other Clinton administration officials, continued to think that Fox should not insist on including immigration in the two countries' relationship, at least not in such a radically different fashion from what had been business as usual. Davidow was especially reluctant: like almost all career diplomats everywhere, he thought things should be left well enough alone, and that, in dealing with Washington, Mexico should stick to the traditional issues and approaches that had functioned appropiately well over the previous ten years: drug enforcement, specific trade questions, border issues, fighting organized crime, etc.

This view simply ignored who Fox was, and what he and his team thought rightly or wrongly their advent to power meant for Mexico. I made the mistake, several months later, of personally asking President Bush to retain Davidow for at least a year into the two new administrations, thinking—erroneously, as it turned out—that his experience in and knowledge of Mexico would be helpful, given the inevitable greenness in both foreign-policy teams. In fact, Davidow remained at his post through the end of the summer of 2002. We all had supposed, after a September 5th dinner at Blair House in Washington during Fox's state visit to the U.S. capital, that George Bush had asked his friend Tony Garza to succeed the career diplomat. Why else would Garza accompany his president at a small dinner attended, on the U.S. side, only by Colin Powell, Condoleezza Rice, Andrew Card, and Karen Hughes? Davidow's distaste for the immigration issue was not decisive in complicating matters, but it was certainly not helpful.

Building on the report made public in mid-2000 by a binational task force sponsored by the Carnegie Endowment for International Peace and the Mexican Autonomous Technological Institute, co-chaired by former Clinton chief of staff Thomas "Mack" McLarty and by former Mexican deputy foreign minister Andrés Rozental, Vicente Fox called for a major overhaul of Mexico's immigration approach, and challenged Washington, and by December, president-elect George W. Bush, to match his own vision and boldness. The report was titled "Mexico-U.S. Migration: A Shared Responsibility," and was essentially premised on the principle that the two nations could not continue simultaneously to be partners on economic matters, and antagonists on immigration issues. It explicitly called for negotiations on migration issues between the two governments, concluded that business as usual was no longer viable, and spelled out many of the specific components of a "Comprehensive Migration Proposal."

The panel, which comprised academics, labor and religious leaders, politicians and businessmen from both countries, stated unambiguously that "the long history of the U.S.-immigration relationship justifies a special bilateral arrangement." It called for a grand bargain made up of four components: "improving the treatment of Mexican migrants by making legal visas and legal status more widely available; helping to reduce unauthorized migration by cooperatively cracking down on criminal smuggling organizations and saving lives by preventing dangerous border crossings; jointly building a viable border region; and targeting development initiatives to areas of high out-migration and strengthening the Mexican economy." The first component was evidently the crucial one. The panel spelled out exactly what it meant: "Convert unauthorized workers into legal temporary workers and provide mechanisms for those who can meet reasonable criteria to earn legal permanent residence status if they wish to do so"; "offer long-term undocumented populations immediate legal permanent resident status"; and "negotiate a temporary labor program." For the incoming Fox administration, the task force report constituted a strong foundation for a radical change in Mexico's stance on immigration, and a well-constructed base for making an immigration agreement with the United States the centerpiece of its new foreign policy. So strong that, as we shall see below, the same basic components would constantly resurface in other documents, reports, and bills or proposals put forth exclusively by Americans for Americans, whether in the Senate, in think tanks or in Executive Branch memos or discussions.

In early January of 2001, barely a month after being appointed Mexico's foreign minister, I sustained an extended, friendly, and highly substantive conversation with Condoleezza Rice, just designated president-elect Bush's national security adviser, on a transcontinental flight from Washington to Los Angeles. The conversation turned into a more formal—though strictly private—one-on-one meeting at LAX Airport for an additional two hours. During those seven hours of uninterrupted exchange, in addition to being able to appreciate Dr. Rice's grace and knowledge of international affairs, Soviet history, and American foreign policy, I was able to sketch out with her what we both hoped would be the basic road map of U.S.-Mexican relations for the coming years. The fundamental issues were divided into several clusters: drug-enforcement and cooperation; border matters, including water rights, infrastructure, combating organized crime, and U.S.-Mexican cooperation on environmental matters; trade, reduced to specific matters like avocados, cement, sugar, and tuna; third-country issues, such as the situation in several Latin American nations, particularly Cuba, Colombia, and Venezuela; multilateral cooperation at the Organization of American States and the United Nations on questions ranging from development financing to human rights and democracy; and, of course, immigration. In contrast to what U.S. critics and Fox's successors would later claim, this was a broad, multifaceted agenda, bearing no resemblance whatsoever to the caricature of a single-issue immigration-obsessed program.

On many of these issues, real progress would be achieved over the next six years, i.e., for the duration of the Fox administration. They ranged from micro, highly specialized issues, to broad definitions of international development. As already stated, the pernicious and nasty drug-enforcement certification process was eliminated; before, every spring, the U.S. administration would pressure (some said blackmail) many countries, among them Mexico, to do more on drug-enforcement, or else the U.S. Congress would "decertify" Mexico and force the executive to suspend aid for drug enforcement (actually, in the case of Mexico, very little money indeed). Mexico would offer up some form of modern-day human sacrifice—a drug lord, a corrupt general, a criminal police commander—and the whole affair would blow over, but not before a great deal of mudslinging and mutual recriminations poisoned relations between the two countries.

Similarly, Mexico and the United States worked well and constructively at the United Nations in forging the so-called Monterrey Consensus, which at the March 2002 conference held in the northern Mexican city of the same name, would establish the framework of international development cooperation for years to come. To a large extent, the Bush Administration's decision to reverse the decade-old decline in U.S. official aid for development (OAD) in poor countries was a result of the conference being hosted by Mexico: on the one hand Bush could hardly not attend a summit of sixty-five heads of state and government scheduled right next door; on the other hand, he couldn't arrive empty-handed. The result was not only the U.S. change of policy—increasing aid instead of reducing it—but also the possibility, for the first time since the 1960s, of an international consensus on development. The rich countries would help the poor ones, but the latter had to adhere to generally accepted norms and principles of governance—respect for human rights, democracy, anti-corruption practices—usually identified with the former. The promises of Bush's Challenge Account have remained unfulfilled, and clearly other priorities have replaced OAD, though U.S. HIV/AIDS support in Africa has grown remarkably under a conservative administration. Still, after years of confrontation on the issue of North-South relations, Mexico and the United States finally reached some common ground.

Likewise, at the Organization of American States, the two countries joined with others to finalize the drafting and signing of the Inter-American Democratic Charter, which at long last began to create a consensus in the region on the need for democratic rule, and the collective nature of the attempt to bring it about and consolidate it. Washington did not support Mexico's subsequent effort to revamp the entire Inter-American security framework, largely because Mexico withdrew from the Rio Treaty or Inter-American Mutual Assistance Treaty in 2002, but in general the two countries worked increasingly well together on hemispheric issues.

At a totally different level of importance, regional and seasonal restrictions slapped years ago on Mexican avocado exports from Michoacán were finally lifted. Sales boomed, jumping from $20 million per year in 2000, to more than $210 million in 2005, a clear example of the possible links between trade; competitive, modernized agriculture; and immigration. All avocados in Mexico worthy of the name come from the town of Uruapán, Michoacán, the southwestern center of the second largest "sending state" in Mexico. But avocados are a highly protected crop in the United States: California has imposed seasonal, phytosanitary, and geographical restrictions on imports from abroad for decades, while at the same time allowing undocumented migrants from Mexico to harvest the protected crops. Some conservative think tanks, such as the Manhattan Institute and its cutting-edge associate Tamar Jacoby, have it right in relation to stoop labor in general—and clearly applicable to avocados in particular—though one can draw opposing conclusions from their conclusion: "The question is whether we want to import more produce from abroad, or more workers from abroad to pick our produce." The long term tendency is clear: two separate agricultural regions are integrating into a single one. But for now, with crops as varied as oranges, avocados, strawberries, tomatoes, cane sugar, etc., it has proved easier for the American political system to tolerate illegal immigration than to eliminate protectionist barriers that would undoubtedly obliterate many activities—agricultural, meatpacking, and others—by transferring them abroad. Or, as some might say, you can't have your avocado and eat it too.

Other issues on the bilateral agenda that Rice and I discussed at LAX did not move forward. Sugar and corn-syrup issues were never really resolved; the North American Development Bank, founded together with NAFTA to fund infrastructure and environmental projects at the border, was never really relaunched; Mexico's water debt to the United States was only reduced when it finally began to rain three years later. This was a terribly delicate issue for George W. Bush, to which he devoted more time and attention than to many others. The reason was simple: he had deep roots in the Rio Grande Valley in Texas, where the water question was an important part of everyday life. Mexico and the United States had signed a water use and limits treaty back in 1944, regulating how the water of two basins—the Colorado River Basin in the west, and the Rio Grande River Basin in the east—would be shared. The treaty was a good deal for Mexico, since all told, Mexico receives four times more water than it gives, but that proportion does not hold true in the Rio Grande Basin. What with drought, corruption in the doling out of water-use permits and the cultivation of water-intensive crops on the Mexican side—walnuts in Chihuahua, for example—Mexico had not been delivering its yearly quota to Texan farmers for several years, thus building up a debt that Bush very much wanted his home constituents to know he was trying to collect on.

On a broader and more visionary note, the very notion of using U.S. and Canadian financial resources to shrink the gap between the poorer member of NAFTA and the two richer ones, along European Union lines (as in the case of Ireland, Spain, Portugal, and Greece in the 1970s and 1980s) never really got off the ground. The idea advanced by the task force mentioned above, of channeling monies to sending communities in Mexico and developing their economies, simply was too anathema for a conservative, antistatist team like Bush's. Moreover, a great deal of the regional and multilateral convergence of those initial months foundered on the shoals of the Iraq invasion two years later.

But immigration suffered a different fate. Until August of 2001, talks, substance, and atmospherics advanced surprisingly fast, and the United States accepted ideas that were totally heretic by previous standards. The main one, of course, was that the issue of migration from Mexico to the United States, and U.S. policy in its regard, was a legitimate bilateral issue, not a U.S. domestic issue that was nobody's business but "America's." This was first laid out in the joint statement by presidents Vicente Fox and George W. Bush, "Towards a Joint Partnership for Prosperity," on February 16, 2001, in Guanajuato, less than a month after Bush's inauguration, on his initial trip abroad. It was the first time that the first presidential trip was to Mexico, not to Canada or the United Kingdom, which understandably had the British and the Canadians quite upset. In its third paragraph, the text clearly said:

> Migration is one of the major ties that bind our societies. It is important that our policies reflect our values and needs, and that we achieve progress in dealing with this phenomenon. We believe that Mexico should make the most of its skills and productivity of their workers at home, and we agree there should be an orderly framework for migration that ensures humane treatment, legal security and dignified labor conditions. For this purpose, *we are instructing our Governments to engage at*

*the earliest opportunity, in formal high-level negotiations aimed
at achieving short and long term agreements that will allow us to
constructively address migration and labor issues between our two
countries.* (author's emphasis)

Many observers later denied that there had been a *real* agreement to negotiate migration accords, or that the United States
ever really meant what it said. Both speculations are credible,
but it would appear difficult for any foreign government, Mexican or otherwise, to imagine that such an explicit and direct
commitment as the one formulated in this communiqué could
be made so lightly.

The joint communiqué issued after the first meeting of the
above-mentioned High-Level Working Group, on April 4, in
Washington, was even more explicit and detailed. It read:

The governments of Mexico and the United States today began
talks intended to achieve a framework for orderly, legal, safe
and humane migration and for the protection of worker
rights. . . . Both governments view this process as an exercise
of shared responsibility, with a long term perspective, to ensure
that migration of Mexicans to the United States is of mutual
opportunity and benefit. Both governments are also committed
to the regulation and safety of persons at our common border. It
is recognized that the components of the agenda form a single
undertaking, seeking an in-depth solution on migration. The first
round of talks established the mechanics of the talks and
a timetable for future activities, as well as the parameters of this
binational effort. The officials of both countries exchanged points
of view concerning short-, medium-, and long-term objectives,
as well as an initial analysis of the actions that might be under-

taken by the executive and legislative branches of each country. The agenda includes discussion of border safety, the H2 visa program, ideas on regularization of undocumented Mexicans in the United States, possible alternatives for temporary workers with an emphasis on circularity, worker rights and labor demand, cooperation on law enforcement issues, regional economic development, and the scheduling of future meetings of the high level working group on migration. The working group will deliver a preliminary report to the Binational Commission meeting to be held this summer. Moreover, the group will endeavor to produce its initial results by the fall of this year and report to our two presidents.

The lengthy quotation gives the lie to any version regarding the nonexistence of a commitment to negotiate, or to move forward, on the issue.

This was an almost astonishing change in U.S. policy, so much so that many people didn't take it seriously. In addition, it would prove to be short-lived and unfruitful. Yet this does not detract from its importance and promise; it simply begs an explanation, rather than an offhand dismissal. What may have occurred was that Colin Powell, who was truly interested in the migration issue, and Dr. Rice, whose interest in all matters Mexican seemed less than central, did not really grasp what they were getting into when they embarked upon this venture. Which was quite logical: for the newly appointed Mexican team, these were issues that had been the subject of study, discussion, and work for years; there is nothing anywhere near as important in Mexican international affairs as the relationship with the country's neighbor to the north; there is nothing today as important in that relationship as immigration. Conversely, neither Powell nor Rice had any experience in dealing with Mexico, the State Department appointments were unmanned for much of that year, or were in the hands of holdovers from before (Davidow himself, assistant under secretary of state for Latin America Pete Romero), and even the domestic political implications of Bush's initial acquiescence to and enthusiasm for the deal with Mexico were unclear.

From many of President Fox's conversations with Bush that I sat in on during those months running up to 9/11, it was evident to me at least that the link between the different facets of the issue was not entirely clear to President Bush. He seemed unaware of the magnitude of the political capital he would have to invest in order to secure any type of agreement both with Mexico and with Democrats and Republicans in Congress. Without these agreements, no arrangement was conceivable. I continue to believe that Bush, Powell, and Rice acted in good faith with Mexico in the course of that period, and that it was only in early August of that year, on the eve of President Fox's trip to Washington and before 9/11, that they began to backtrack as a result of their greater awareness of exactly what they had committed themselves to. Bush became engaged for many reasons, ranging from his own personal acquaintance with the issue, to his Texan, pro-immigrant, pro-Mexican experience. In addition, he clearly possessed the conviction, together with Karl Rove, that in the long run the Republican Party needed Latino votes, and that an anti-immigrant posture, such as former California governor Pete Wilson's back in 1992 on Proposition 187, seeking to deny schools and basic emergency health services to people without papers, was political suicide. Bush himself did better among Latinos in the 2000 election than any Republican had done before, and he knew that over time the

Hispanic vote would become increasingly crucial in many states, not just Texas, California, Illinois, and New York.

As the American administration began to realize what it had gotten itself into, it searched for wiggle room. A mini-crisis exploded a month before President Fox's state visit to Washington in early September. In a one-on-one conversation I had with Powell, with no staff in the room, I learned Bush was a bit upset at me for "getting out ahead of the president," partly because Fox had uttered many statements on immigration during a tour of the Midwest in July, partly because I had made a speech to a group of hotel-worker union officials in Los Angeles where I coined the phrase "the whole enchilada" as a synonym for what we wanted. This led Washington to table a proposal—informally, of course—that it knew was unacceptable, not only to us but also to Democrats in Congress: a guest-worker program with 250,000 visas per year, but no provisions for legalization for Mexicans already in the United States. As such, Fox would have been slammed in Mexico had he even entertained such a notion, but in fact this was a sign that the United States did want some sort of coming together of minds on the issue, even if it had still not thought the entire matter through.

Fox's trip to Washington was highly successful, by traditional U.S.-Mexican standards. Huge media attention; a White House gala dinner with fireworks on the Mall; many meetings with congressional leaders; excellent rapport between the principals and their aides; a flight on Air Force One to Ohio for a Fox-Bush public event (that many of the Mexicans in Butler County, mentioned in Chapter One, attended); a Fox speech to the OAS proclaiming Mexico's abrogation of the Rio Treaty (which the Americans did not like but which gave Fox cover in Mexico for upcoming rapprochements with Washington): even the most critical Mexican press was forced to acknowledge that never before had a Mexican president been received that well in the American capital. Moreover, and most important, many of the immigration misunderstandings were thrashed out. According to the joint communiqué issued after the meetings, "the deliberations reflected *the most frank and productive dialogue that had ever taken place* over such a relevant issue [migration] for both nations" (author's emphasis). Fox's meetings with Bush, a major speech he gave to a joint session of Congress, and the brave stance adopted by Secretary of State Colin Powell—rejecting Attorney General John Ashcroft's and the Domestic Policy Staff's hard line—placed things back on the right track . . . for three days, until September 11, 2001. From that day until early 2006, nothing really happened; and then it seemed, for a while, that a deal—different from the one originally fleshed out, but which included many of its components—was feasible.

The essence of the quid pro quos or trade-offs that Mexico put on the table, first at meetings between Colin Powell and myself, then during President Bush's visit to Vicente Fox's home in Guanajuato, and subsequently at two working sessions in April and August of the High-Level Migration Working Group set up by both governments, was in fact quite simple. It would continue to figure at the heart of Mexico's immigration stance throughout the Fox term and, indeed, at the heart of the entire immigration debate in the United States. Fox summed it up in his White House lawn speech that September, in what some considered an ultimatum to Bush ("We should get a deal by year's end") and others as simply an emphasis on urgency and a demonstration of willingness to negotiate flexibly.

The first trade-off mainly involved U.S. domestic politics, the other domestic Mexican politics. On the northern side of the border, thanks to the presence in the previously mentioned task force of Catholic Church hierarchs and labor and Latino leaders—such as Eliseo Medina from the Service Employees International Union in the AFL-CIO and Antonia Hernández from Mexican-American Legal Defense Fund (MALDEF)—and to countless conversations held by Fox and his aides with Americans across the political spectrum, it had become obvious that any deal necessarily comprised two ingredients. One implicated Mexicans already in the United States, or what could be called the *stock* question; the other implied the future of Mexicans who over the next fifteen years—until demographics settled the question by having the Mexican population age so much it simply would cease to emigrate, regardless of economics—would continue to migrate north, or what could be called the *flow* question. From the very beginning of the two administrations, it became obvious that in the United States, the Catholic Church, Latinos, and labor were opposed, on occasion adamantly, to any form of guest-worker program as the only solution to the flow question. Fox met with AFL-CIO president John Sweeney at the Davos World Economic Summit in January 2001, and he heard in no uncertain terms that the American labor movement was extremely skeptical about such programs, either the U.S. version—the Bracero Agreement—or the European style of *gastarbeiter* schemes. The Latino leaders Fox spoke with, along with liberal Democratic members of Congress like Richard Gephardt, Christopher Dodd, and Edward Kennedy, were also reluctant, as was the U.S. Catholic Church, particularly Roger Cardinal Mahoney of Los Angeles.

Their motivations were generally altruistic and understandable. The peril of creating a permanent foreign underclass of low-skilled, low-wage, low-education laborers, was real. Labor rights have never been enforced as rigorously in the United States as in Western Europe, for example; giving U.S. business access to low-salary employees, without rights, without protection, without access to permanent residence in the United States, which seemed to fly in the face of everything American liberals believed in. The virtual debt-peonage that many thought the Bracero Agreement had introduced north of the border was a repulsive precedent; the situation of Turks in Germany, Indonesians in Holland, and Yugoslavians in Sweden were all cast in a similar light. Furthermore, the possibilities of organizing and eventually registering the guest workers to vote appeared illusory, when not frankly impossible. Thus, without a road to citizenship, with workers coming from and going home every six months, speaking no English, having no time to learn it, possessing pitifully low educational levels, what could labor, Latinos, and liberals possibly gain from a guest-worker program?

What this estate of American society hoped for was something totally different, diametrically opposed to a guest-worker program: the process then known as amnesty, whereby everyone already in the United States (with some restrictions and requirements) could obtain residence and then citizenship with time, patience, and some money. This side—the stock side—of the political/immigration equation was largely indifferent to the other side, the flow side: what about those who had not yet arrived, but who undoubtedly would? The bridge to the end of immigration from Mexico was real, but long: it would be another ten to fifteen years before the pool of young, potential emigrants from Mexico would shrink sufficiently through demographic transition to dry up. In the meantime, whatever else occurred, people would continue to drift northward. The liberal left had little to say about this.

Conversely, the huge change on the business, conservative, Republican side of the aisle represented by the acceptance of—or enthusiasm for—a guest-worker program was compensated for by a rabid rejection of anything sounding like amnesty, i.e., the only solution, disguised or otherwise, to the stock question. Thanks to statements like Alan Greenspan's, as a result of the booming economy and of ensuing, expanding demand for low-wage labor, and because business interests close to the Republican Party wanted access to that labor, right-of-center members of Congress ranging from archconservatives like senators Phil Gramm of Texas and Jesse Helms of North Carolina, to Republican moderates like Senator Pete Domenici of New Mexico or representatives Bill Cannon of Utah and Jeff Flake of Arizona all came out, early in the Bush administration's term, in favor of a guest-worker program.

True enough, they were somewhat uncomfortable with it, wondering if the guests would actually go home when their invitation expired. They did not define clearly or exactly what they meant by it, and left many questions unanswered. Would it be an expansion of the existing H2A and H2B seasonal worker programs? Would it apply only to agriculture, or also to services and industry in general? What did "temporary" or "guest" actually signify? Would it involve "only" Mexico, or "first" Mexico, and subsequently other countries? Was there a path to permanent-resident status and then citizenship, and would Mexicans without proper papers already in the United States be eligible for it? They had no answers for any of these questions, in the same way the Democrats really knew very little about what to do, for example, with existing guest-worker programs that invited more than 70,000 Mexicans every year to the United States for six months or more. Indeed, since 1992 the U.S. consulate in Monterrey had begun extending temporary worker visas—in agriculture, labeled H2A, and in services and industry, known as H2B. Between 1995 and 2000 the number of H2As jumped from 7,099 to 26,902; the H2Bs from 1,225 to 20,057. By 2005 the total for both was nearly 75,000; this was roughly five times the size of the guest-worker program Mexico had signed years ago with Canada. So the Democrats rejected something that already existed, and the Republicans didn't want what their last real hero—Ronald Reagan—had signed into law in 1986: amnesty. Moreover, though the exact numbers were hard to come by, there appeared to be scant leakages from these programs: most of those let in went home. The reason was simple: the "guests" had a credible guarantee that they would be allowed back in the following year, part of their wages were withheld until their departure, and they *wanted* to return to their families, their communities, and their country.

What was amnesty, at the time? It was basically viewed through the prism of IRCA and the 1986 pardon and legalization it immediately provided, eventually to 2.3 million Mexicans and 700,000 additional immigrants from other lands, without deterring further immigration to the smallest extent. It meant, as the catchphrases went, "rewarding those who broke the law," "punishing those who wait patiently in line in their home countries," letting millions of immigrants in through subsequent family reunification. In fact, in addition to the 1.3 million legalized directly through IRCA's amnesty provisions, another 1.1 million Mexicans were legalized through the Special Agricultural Worker (SAW) provisions, and possibly as many as another 1.5 million Mexicans were indirectly legalized, thanks to family reunification in subsequent years. And perhaps most important, as President Bush confessed to President Fox in Guanajuato in February 2001, it meant a very considerable number of Democratic voters ten years down the line. With the exception of Cuban Americans in Florida and New Jersey, most Hispanic voters in the United States voted Democratic, though in 2000 they had voted in a larger proportion for George Bush in Texas than ever before. But for legal and moral conservatives like John Ashcroft, Bush's first attorney general and many others of a similar persuasion, the fundamental objection to amnesty was that it violated a basic tenet of the rule of law.

Both sides of the debate in the United States had valid points, and also lacked answers to valid questions. The points would begin to be addressed during the first eight months of negotiations, but the answers would be forthcoming much more slowly. As was already stated, however, the main accomplishment for Mexico lay in the fact that Washington had apparently accepted something inconceivable just months before: to negotiate its immigration policy with another country. Paradoxically, this had only occurred, in fact and in significant numbers, with Fidel Castro's Cuba. Since the early 1960s, and as late as 1994, successive U.S. administrations had negotiated visa quotas with the island regime; as some said, Washington was willing to do this with its worst enemy but not with its neighbor. So to suddenly see that immigration had become a legitimate topic of negotiation, even if the disagreements in its regard seemed abysmal, was quite a surprise. I recall how in the negotiations of the above-cited press communiqué for the Bush visit to Mexico in February 2001, my deputy, Enrique Berruga, was amazed to watch the American side accept practically everything the Mexican side wanted. It wouldn't last.

Mexican politics were also complicated, and the risks Fox took were greater than Bush's, though at the time, and even now, this was not readily apparent. Mexico had traditionally opposed any kind of cooperation with the United States on immigration for two reasons. The first involved the bitter aftertaste left by the Bracero Agreement; as I have already explained, most Mexican scholars thought it had been humiliating for Mexico. According to conventional wisdom, any immigration agreement with the United States would inexorably reproduce the worst vices and defects of the 1942–64 arrangement. So by simply saying he wanted an agreement, Fox was going out on a limb; Bush sawed it off.

But more important, any immigration deal inescapably implied a Mexican commitment regarding the so-called remaining undocumented flows. Suppose an agreement was reached on guest workers that provided around an additional 250,000 temporary visas for Mexicans per year—raising the total to 325,000, a very acceptable number at the time—and that all of the other problems related to such a program were adequately addressed. The number of Mexicans leaving their country in 2001 without papers was approximately 400,000; the hypothetical program would not cover everybody. Thus, in addition to the quarter of a million new, legal temporary workers, somewhat less than another 100,000 would continue to leave illegally. What was Mexico going to do about it? Persist in its ostrichlike approach, claiming that this was not its problem, and that furthermore the Mexican Constitution forbade any restrictions on freedom of circulation within the country? Would Mexico keep on insisting that it could materially not stop anyone from departing, if only because the first to leave would be the policemen or soldiers stationed at the border with the purpose of closing it off to unlawful exits? And what would it do to finally, effectively, deter other countries' immigrants (known as OTMs, other than Mexicans) from using Mexico as a conduit to the United States? Or would it finally step up to the plate and acknowledge that its own immigration legislation made exits legal only at predetermined points and with preestablished Mexican papers, and that there was a great deal it could do to seal its southern border and work in the sending communities to discourage unauthorized departures and encourage people without permits to stay home?

For Fox, this was conceptually one of the most difficult decisions of his six-year term. He forcefully came down on the side of setting aside Mexico's traditional stance, and committing himself, with George Bush, to share responsibility for these remaining flows, once an overall understanding was reached. He never had to deliver on his commitment, because Bush never delivered on a deal; his successor is not bound by it legally, since it was never inscribed in a treaty. But it was the most important concession Fox was to make to the United States during his presidency, and it will probably stand, if only because it is an absolute precondition for any immigration agreement between the two countries or for Mexican cooperation with the United States on immigration reform enacted by the U.S. Congress. Had the Mexican opposition understood at the time what Fox was promising, it would have raised hell; this had been an absolute taboo in Mexico for decades. By the time it figured it out in 2005, the commitment and its enormous significance had been assimilated at least by part of that opposition.

The key question in this process, as it would be five years later in the U.S. congressional debate on immigration reform, was exactly what "Comprehensive Reform," or a "single understanding" or the "whole enchilada," actually meant for both countries. In fact, there was very little leeway for diverging interpretations. For Mexico, it implied that, short of an overall package, it could not even begin to think about shared responsibility; for the United States, it meant that there was no conceivable deal with the Congress that did not address both sides of the issue—amnesty and guest workers—because the votes were simply not available only on one side of the aisle, and the other side would never go along with its pet peeves if it did not get its pet projects. This was the dimension of the immigration negotiations on the eve of 9/11; as we shall see below, on the substance, not much has changed, but the climate has, though no one knows if for better or for worse.

As shown, then, the four criticisms generally leveled at Mexico for this period do not entirely hold water. First, Washington clearly agreed and committed itself to negotiating an immigration agreement with Mexico, and the negotiations actually got under way; whether they would have come to fruition without 9/11 is an imponderable question. Moreover, Washington has negotiated immigration agreements with other countries in the past, most notably Cuba in 1994. Second, Mexico knew full well that any deal reached with the executive would have to be approved by Congress, which was why, literally from the first days of the Fox administration, either the president or the foreign minister held meetings in Washington and Mexico City with leading senators and, to a lesser extent, House members. Practically the entire Senate Foreign Relations Committee, including its then-chairman and PRI nemesis Jesse Helms (who prided himself on rarely visiting other nations), traveled to Mexico in Januay 2001. I met with House Majority Leader Dick Gephardt in Mexico on three occasions (in Mexico City, Cuernavaca, and Acapulco), and Fox not only addressed a full session of Congress on his state visit to Washington in September 2001, but also subsequently met at length with a group of more than twenty senators the following day. Third, despite insinuations to the contrary, immigration was by no means the only issue on the bilateral agenda, as defined by Mexico or by Washington; at least as much time was devoted to water, drug-enforcement certification, Venezuela and specific trade issues during the pre-9/11 period, and to security and the United Nations after 9/11. Finally, the question remains: should Mexico have lobbied as hard and as publicly as it did during the first two years of the Fox term, with as high a profile as it acquired in the U.S. national and local media? The results are inconclusive: "going public" got the immigration issue on the agenda, where it has remained ever since, and built coalitions of support for it, but it also generated resistance (though much of that probably preexisted); Bush's hands-off discretion recommendation after 2004, in particular, brought meager results. Many countries use the U.S. bully pulpit in the United States; why should Mexico refrain from doing so?

FIVE

Many observers concluded that, regardless of whether 9/11 was a cause or merely a pretext for the indefinite postponement of the migration negotiations, Mexico reacted too slowly to the new era ushered in by the terrorist attack. They thought, on the one hand, that Mexico should have quickly shelved its emphasis on immigration in the bilateral relationship; and on the other, somewhat contradictorily, that immigration would only fly if it was packaged together with a significant security component. On the first point, the proof that once the cat was out of the bag, it was politically suicidal for Mexico to retreat from putting immigration front and center on its international agenda, was that my successor in the Foreign Ministry, who never shared that view and did not agree with that emphasis, was unable to walk away from it; nor could Fox's successor, Felipe Calderón, leave the issue alone or de-emphasize it, despite all the advice and entreaties that he received to that effect. The fate of the now nearly 12 million Mexican citizens in the United States, and of the 350,000 to 400,000 that continue to leave every year, is Mexico's most important foreign-policy item, whether its leaders like it or not.

On the question of security, the fact is that Mexico did then exactly what Fox's critics suggested much later. The problem was that the security issue did not take initially, although on paper, it seemed to be a natural complement to immigration after 9/11. The Mexican authorities thought from Day One of the post-9/11 world that the best and probably only way to salvage what had been achieved in the migration talks and maintain momentum was to link immigration with security: U.S. security, North American security, international security. This was much more the result of political expediency and potential pandering to White House sensitivities than real conviction about the factual foundation for the linkage. Most Mexicans in official positions—and indeed many Americans—simply did not believe that there was a causal, real-world link between immigration and security. Public opinion in the United States was not especially concerned; for example, in an April 2006 Fox News poll, only 34 percent of those interviewed were very concerned that illegal immigration would increase terrorism—this in a survey carried out by a virulently anti-immigration-reform news organization. According to an NPR/Kaiser/Kennedy School poll conducted in mid-2004, when the memory of 9/11 had not yet faded as much, not more than 56 percent of nonimmigrants thought "illegal immigration increased the threat of terrorism."

Migrants from Mexico, legal or otherwise, were not al-Qaeda operatives in disguise; the latter were not going to pass as expatriates from the Sierra Mixteca and enter the United States that way. And if they did want to use Mexico as a stepping stone to the United States, they could do so legally, like the nineteen Saudis who brought down the World Trade Center towers: given certain economic conditions, it remains relatively easy to obtain a visa to enter the United States as a tourist. If there was a link, it stemmed from political considerations: as I stated at a meeting of the U.S. Senate Foreign Relations Committee in 2005—two years after having resigned as foreign minister—whatever cooperation Mexico could provide the United States, and regardless of how important or relevant that cooperation could be, depended on the United States reciprocating on a materially unlinked, but politically indissociable, issue: immigration. Conversely, I pointed out, the United States would never be able to acquiesce to Mexico's demands on immigration, unless a deal included a significant security element, at least for political cover.

Thus at a preparatory, undersecretary-level meeting for a summit scheduled for March 22, 2002, and held in Washington on January 28 of that year between Mexican officials and INS commissioner James Ziglar, who was accompanied by the late senior State Department official Mary Ryan, the Mexicans clearly stated to their counterparts, under direct instructions from Mexico City. "For the Government of Mexico a detailed security cooperation agreement such as the one the United States was proposing could only be acceptable if it included the migration issue; that is, if the agreement contained an explicit link saying that security cooperation was founded and justified because it was part of a migratory solution." The American officials acknowledged that it was their job (State and INS) to convince other U.S. government agencies that "the equation was simple: there can be no cooperation on security without the migration component and vice versa." The connection was indeed purely political, because in real life, it did not exist.

This was perhaps the weak point of the linkage argument, and why it did not fly. Mary Ryan, by the way, who was at that point the second most senior career ambassador in the U.S. Foreign Service, was soon fired ignominiously by her superiors. As the assistant undersecretary in charge of consular affairs, she was hauled in before higher-echelon officials after 9/11 to explain how and why the nineteen perpetrators of the terrorist attacks had all entered the country with proper visas: what happened? She and her colleagues fine-combed the full dossiers of each visa applicant; they concluded—and demonstrated—that existing procedures had been followed perfectly in eighteen of the nineteen cases, and no one was responsible for the tragedy: everyone had done his or her job properly, but the Saudi jihadists had simply outsmarted an imperfect system. She was nonetheless made the scapegoat in front of Congress, who needed someone to blame; together with Colin Powell, she was Mexico's best ally in this process.

Fox had in fact brought up the security issue with Bush in their first talk after 9/11, at the White House on October 4, 2001, and repeatedly during his conversations with the U.S. leader throughout the United Nations Summit on Development Financing, held in Monterrey, Mexico, in late March 2002. At that meeting, in the course of a separate, bilateral encounter between the two presidents, the two countries signed the Border Partnership Agreement (or "Smart Border Agreement") that included twenty-two specific points on border issues, ports of entry, exchange of information, etc. But although Mexico repeatedly stressed that the best way to enhance U.S. security was both to bring people out of the shadows, and to allow them into the United States legally and securely, the Bush administration was not buying. It seemed to think two different things about the security question with Mexico, both of which made any correlation idle or needless. First, as mentioned above, the Bush crew doubted that there was a real security threat to the United States from across the border with Mexico or from Mexicans in the United States; it simply did not believe—and was almost certainly right—that terrorists, al-Qaeda operatives, or foreign government agents hostile to the United States would enter from Mexico. They had not before 9/11; they haven't since, as of this writing. Consequently, while cooperation with Mexico seemed useful, it was not deemed worthy of major concessions, and particularly not on such a delicate issue as immigration. Second, Washington seemed persuaded—again, correctly—that Mexico would furnish pretty much any necessary cooperation without asking for much in return.

Nonetheless, Mexico insisted on the security component, essentially to placate what it thought were bona fide American concerns. At the first meeting of the Mexican-U.S. technical group on migration (that reported to the High-Level Group created at the Guanajuato Summit, February 2001) after 9/11, on November 20, 2001, the two sides agreed that the security issue had become essential. They then included specific security issues in the technical group's agenda.* And although, as we just saw, the INS commissioner acknowledged at that meeting that Mexico could not deliver on security without getting something on immigration, he stressed the need to maintain this matter under the greatest confidentiality and discretion, since he thought there would be opposition to the idea on the part of the DPC (Domestic Policy Council) in the White House. And even a year later, during a meeting of the Binational Commission in Mexico City (the last one I co-chaired with Colin Powell) the joint draft communiqué stated: "Migration continues to be a key

---

*The text explicitly stated that "after the 9-11 attacks the security issue had acquired an unprecedented importance for the group. They decided to include in the technical group's agenda issues such as exchange of information, experience and practices on migratory laws and visas for third country nationals, as well as considering the adoption of complementary measures in consular and immigration procedures for third country nationals, in order to prevent the presence of possible terrorists on Mexican or US soil."

bilateral issue, although the events of September 11th, made the working group include joint cooperation on border security. . . . The U.S.-Mexico Border partnership reflects the priority both countries place on security matters."

In fact, Mexico tried to convince the other U.S. border neighbor to participate in this process, through what diplomats call trilateral talks. I met with Canada's deputy prime minster in charge of security matters, John Manley (a good friend and colleague from years past), in New York in early October 2001 for that purpose. Unfortunately, I got nowhere on this issue, as on so many others with Canada: Ottawa simply and perhaps understandably has never wanted to share its privileged relationship with Washington with anyone else. As Manley perhaps a bit undiplomatically but logically replied to my entreaties, "We don't want to contaminate our border with them with yours."

In the end, Mexico was unwilling to sustain the link between immigration and security, partly because of U.S. unresponsiveness, partly because the responsibility for negotiating the Monterrey March 22nd twenty-two-point agreement on security, was assigned to Interior Minister Santiago Creel instead of the Foreign Ministry, and Creel wanted a nonconflicting deal with the Americans. On the U.S. side, Homeland Security was the interlocutor; on the Mexican side, it could have been either Interior—in charge of intelligence and coordinating security issues—or the Foreign Ministry, responsible for all international negotiations except those someone else was responsible for. Charging both with the task begged the question: who would lead? Fox's decision to pick Creel was a perfectly reasonable one, but it implied that domestic political considerations would be paramount and foreign-policy concerns would be absent. So it was. Creel was running to succeed Fox as president in 2006, as I also tried to do, and for that purpose reverted to the traditional Mexican stance in relation to the United States: speak harshly and carry a small stick. He was strident in public, particularly with regard to U.S. Ambassador Tony Garza's comments on violence at the border in 2004–6, but he pretty much caved in on most matters in private with the United States. That was exactly what occurred on security and migration. Mexico essentially gave up on linking the two issues, whereas over time, the Bush administration, and the bipartisan majority that emerged in the Senate, came around to the view that the two had to go together, for questionable intrinsic, substantive reasons, but also in view of each country's pragmatic political necessities already described above.

The Bush administration was thus reticent about this connection at the beginning of the post-9/11 era, and, parenthetically, did not even engage itself in another tack the Mexicans tried in mid-2002. This was oil. After a visit by congressional Democratic House and Senate leaders Tom Daschle and Richard Gephardt to Mexico in November 2001, I tried to convince President Fox that there was an oil angle to 9/11. The two Democrats, who met with me and separately, and at length, with Fox, thought that the era of U.S.-energy dependence on Saudi Arabia and the Gulf had come to an end with 9/11. The Saud family, despite its long-standing ties to the United States and to the Bush family, was simply no longer reliable, or the cost of keeping it in line and in power was becoming exorbitant for the United States. Mexico was already the United States' first supplier of oil, slightly ahead of Riyadh and Canada, and could, if helped, become a partial substitute of the roughly 50 percent of American imports streaming in from the Persian Gulf and Venezuela, a region and a country that both seemed, even then, explosive and precarious. The only problem was that expanding Mexican extraction of crude would cost a great deal of money—most of the potential lay in the deep waters of the Gulf of Mexico—Mexico didn't have it, and its Constitution did not permit foreign investment in the industry. One way to square the circle, perhaps, according to Daschle and Gephardt, was to establish long-range supply agreements between the two nations, which would ensure financing—by international lending against future streams, though not reserves—for the expansion of Mexico's production, price guarantees for Mexico, and supply guarantees for the United States. I thought, mistakenly I suppose, that migration could be attached to this. The deal appeared to be very attractive to the United States, entailed responsibilities and opportunities for Mexico (using its increased oil revenues to develop the country), and, with immigration, might be sellable domestically (though the poll quoted earlier in Chapter Four and taken in 2004 suggests otherwise).

Fox was never entirely convinced, but allowed me to broach the subject with Powell and even with Bush directly at the Monterrey bilateral encounters in March 2002. They were not interested; later, when I asked knowledgeable Americans why this was so, the only answers I received were unsatisfactory: the Bush links to Saudi Arabia, the administration was already thinking about Iraq, they didn't believe Mexico could deliver, the Bush team could only deal with one issue at a time. And yet the idea was intriguing; the two excluded issues from NAFTA—immigration and energy—were also the two eight-hundred-pound gorillas in the bilateral agenda room; why not address them together? It wasn't meant to be; the United States is more dependent than ever on unreliable oil; Mexico's production is beginning to decline, and the country is less ready than ever to overhaul its constitutional restrictions (a poll taken in late 2006 on the same issue as before showed that 76 percent of all Mexicans were opposed to permitting foreign investment in oil). And, of course, immigration only really moved forward after the November 2006 midterm elections and the Democrats' victory, and then in ways that could have been significantly improved upon.

Late in 2002, on a visit to Mexico City, Powell confided to me that he seriously doubted there would be any movement on immigration during Bush's first term. His skepticism on what the occupation of Iraq, as opposed to the upcoming invasion, would require and his reluctance to get entangled in it—which I summarized as his unwillingness to be "their McArthur"—all pointed to a prolonged interruption of the migration negotiations. In Powell's view, there would be no deal for Bush's first term. The entire matter became a moot one during all of 2003, because of Iraq, Bush's obsession with it, and Mexico's stance against the invasion at the UN Security Council. Bush dearly wanted Mexico's support, because with it came Chile's and, according to what Powell told me months after the invasion, at least Pakistan's and Angola's, too. Those votes would have awarded Washington the majority it hungered for: nine of the fifteen members. This was a good second-best to a unanimous resolution, since on the one hand it showed that a majority of the council supported the invasion, and it would have obliged France, Russia, or China to use their veto, which they were uncertain about doing.

Mexico's refusal to support Bush was, in my opinion—although I was no longer foreign minister at the time—the appropriate one, directly derived from the foreign policy Fox and I had designed since 1999. Fox refused to knuckle under to Washington's considerable pressure for four reasons. First, public opinion in Mexico was overwhelmingly against the war and opposed to any inkling of Mexican backing for it. And Fox read polls like the Bible. Second, the former president is a profoundly Catholic individual, who deeply believes that wars are simply not willingly entered into. Third, the U.S. case in any of its facets (WMD, Saddam as a worse dictator than others, building democracy in the Arab world, etc.) was not convincing in itself, and much less so as grounds for going against everything the Mexican political elite believed in (though not the business community, which would have liked Fox to go along with Washington). And finally, by then, the Mexican leader was already profoundly disillusioned with Bush, and intuitively felt he would never deliver on his promises, regardless of what Mexico did or did not do; Mexico was not sacrificing an immigration agreement by not backing Bush: it was simply drawing the right conclusion from the self-evident fact that Bush was neither willing nor able to negotiate such an agreement anymore, even if he had been earlier.

Fox tried to finesse the issue by fudging the matter in several phone conversations with Bush; the latter thought Fox was saying yes, the former thought he was politely and diplomatically saying no. Fox probably got it wrong: he should have been explicit in private and ambiguous in public. He did the opposite: unfortunately, midterm elections were scheduled for that summer in Mexico, and Fox was unable to resist the temptation to use his anti-Bush opposition in the Security Council for domestic electoral purposes (to no avail, by the way: Fox's party received a drubbing in the July 2003 legislative vote). He turned up the volume on his criticism of the invasion of Iraq, acknowledged that had there been a vote at the UN, Mexico would have said no, when what Powell was trying to achieve was precisely to avoid forcing countries to take sides, knowing the United States' case was lost anyway. All told, there was no love lost between Bush and Fox during those months, and whatever chances there may have been for some sort of partial, interim agreement on immigration, were lost in the sands of the Iraqi desert.

But during this entire period, whether before 9/11 when there was real momentum; between 9/11 and Iraq, when everything was suspended but not abandoned; or during 2003, a year devoted to Iraq in one way or another, on both sides of the border a great deal of progress was made insofar as understanding the complicated nuts and bolts of the immigration issue. A series of questions were addressed, and a number of answers were conceptualized. They all boiled down to a set of dichotomies: Could there be a temporary or guest-worker program without some form of mass legalization, regularization, or amnesty, regardless of the term one prefers? Could there be any type of path to residence and eventually to citizenship for the now 12 million undocumented migrants in the United States without there also being some type of guest-worker program? How could undocumented aliens already in the United States "fit" into a temporary-worker program? Should immigration be addressed as a bilateral matter with source countries, mainly Mexico, or should it—and could it—return to being a strictly domestic U.S. affair? Was a temporary-worker program possible without source-country cooperation and co-management? And finally, should all of this be for Mexico first, or for Mexico only, or for everybody at the same time? There were no ideal responses to these dilemmas, but there were also few alternatives to the feasible, reasonable, accessible, and imperfect solutions. The narrow leeway for any real exit from the immigration maze made it paradoxically easier to solve: there just were not that many ways out available, and the only real choice was between a comprehensive reform whose basic ingredients were more or less known, or the status quo.

The first dilemma had to do with the perennial, age-old question of amnesty. As internal State and Labor Department documents (generally referred to as non-papers: these were confidential documents exchanged between the two governments, or leaked by our U.S. allies to the Mexican negotiators during the talks, and which did not represent formal, definitive stances but indicated possible avenues of understanding) from 2001 put it: "The Administration must decide whether to develop a temporary-worker program, and whether to establish a means whereby workers in such a program can obtain permanency in the United States. Furthermore, the Administration must decide if, and if so, how to address the issue of undocumented aliens in the United States. The Administration has indicated that it does not support a broad-based amnesty. . . ." So far, so good. The documents stated the formal Bush administration stance: no amnesty. But they also acknowledged the complexity of that position. Accepting that the questions of guest workers and legalization were indissociable, they recognized that most pro-immigration constituencies in the United States were more interested in legalization than in guest workers, while confessing that, without some form of legalization or permanency, undocumented residents in the United States would simply not join a guest-worker program: "Absent a residency component any TWP is unlikely to succeed."*

Herein lay the reasoning behind the Mexican stance—the "whole enchilada"—which later, in 2006, became the formal

---

*The entire paragraph stated: "In today's political climate, the issues of a TWP and 'regularizing' [Mexican term for legalizing] the status of the undocumented aliens in the United States are closely linked. Soundings in Congress and among most interested private sector groups, unions, NGOs, employer associations, etc., reveal that their primary concern is for the administration to address the matter of the undocumented residents of the United States before they would entertain supporting a TWP. Furthermore, a means of granting permanency to workers must be developed or undocumented workers currently in the United States, who may qualify for participation in a TWP, will not likely be motivated to step forward to seek lawful status in the United States."

stance adopted by the White House itself: comprehensive immigration reform. One of the touchier subjects then and now has been whether any Mexican in the United States without papers will emerge from the dark, register, and then leave the country, with the promise that if he waits patiently in line back home for several years, he will eventually return. This was simply not going to occur, and Colin Powell, whose parents were immigrants from Jamaica, understood it full well. No self-respecting Mexican in the United States, who had paid a substantial fee to the coyote to get in, who had a job and a home, whose family had traveled north to join him, and who knew that the chances of being caught and deported were minuscule indeed, was going to willingly commit migratory hara-kiri.

The story of Alicia in New York provides a good example. She arrived in the United States from Mexico City in 2003, after paying a pollero $2,000, staked by her family in Mexico, she was forty years old. Her initial destination was Connecticut, but she ended up doing domestic work in Manhattan, where she makes between $300 and $400 weekly. The saga of her exodus is this: She had just gotten divorced, and lost custody of her children. Their father refused to pay for the elder daughter's education, and Alicia felt she had no choice but go north to fund her daughter Jessica's schooling (she is now studying psychology at a private run-of-the-mill college that nonetheless would be totally out of reach without remittances). She hooked up with a group of sixty people in Altar, south of Sasabe in Sonora, where the migrants were loaded up in a minivan that took them to the border. The van broke down, but the pollero told the group not to get out while they fixed it (it took them two hours in the 120-degree heat) because the desert "was packed with snakes, scorpions, and poisonous weeds." On that first try, she was caught and sent back across the border. The second time she crossed with a group of thirty-five colleagues, mostly men. She was transferred to a jump-off point in the desert "where everybody had to leave everything we were carrying, keeping just water, no backpack, no papers, no nothing," and then undertook the trek through the desert, guided by a single smuggler. She walked for two days to reach the first destination in Arizona, and took another fifteen days, walking and packed into a small truck like a sardine, to her final point of departure to New York.

She crossed together with a friend of her brother's who was supposed to get her to Connecticut, but he dumped Alicia in New York, where she has remained ever since. She has found almost permanent work as a babysitter, housekeeper, and cook for a Mexican diplomat in Manhattan who offered to take her to Washington, having been transferred there by the new Mexican administration. The diplomat even offered Alicia a U.S. visa in Mexico City, through the U.S. embassy there, if she went back to get it. Needless to say, Alicia refused and keeps working in New York, sending her daughter money and Christmas gifts and waiting for amnesty. College costs about $650 per month. With another $100 to $150 for expenses, Alicia sends home $800 a month: a savings rate of 50 percent. She will never leave the United States unless she is absolutely sure she can come back, and that certainty goes beyond promises: Colin Powell's, the Mexican diplomat's, or a U.S. Senate bill's. Moreover, it is likely that there will be more and more Alicias: women from urban or rural areas emigrating to pay for their children's education. Why do we know this? For several reasons.

A poll published in the Mexican public opinion journal *Este País* in November 2006 showed that studying or concluding one's studies is the number two "dream" or "desire" of all Mexicans, regardless of age group, social class, region, or gender. Only the generic answer "personal improvement" scores higher. But education is the choice of more Mexicans from rural areas than from urban ones, for more women than for men, and for more people in the west of the country (where most emigrants still come from) than for the rest. If in addition we recall that education in Mexico, for better or for worse, is gradually privatizing, as public schools continue to deteriorate (35 percent of all higher education students are now enrolled in private institutions; the figure for high school has almost reached 25 percent), and we also remember that there are more and more single mothers in Mexico, the equation is easy to solve. Alicia will become a model: women will emigrate, with or without papers, finding jobs on occasion that men cannot take—health care, housework, babysitting—to finance their offsprings' education, which costs more and more, but is viewed by a growing number of Mexicans from rural, sending areas as the central fixture of the Mexican dream.

The Mexican side on the negotiations attempted to get around the amnesty obstacle by finessing the terminology, and linking the situation of the then roughly 3.5 million Mexicans without papers in the United States to what the Bush people wanted, i.e., a temporary-worker program. As the above mentioned documents stated:

> The term regularization was introduced by the Mexican team and was interpreted to mean a mechanism whereby undocumented aliens in the United States could become legalized under U.S. Immigration Law. . . . The Mexicans clearly and immedi-

ately wanted the talks to address all (the) elements as a whole. The Americans for various reasons saw these as separate issues that had to be addressed accordingly. . . . With regularization seen as unfeasible, immediate attention was given to a TWP. The two countries concurred on a set of principles and a common concept. All parties quickly realized that without addressing regularization first, no advancement could be made on TWP.

This was perhaps the crux of the entire matter then, and remains so today.

The Bush administration initially thought, perhaps persuaded by holdovers in the State Department like U.S. ambassador to Mexico Jeffrey Davidow, who was not part of the Bush team nor was an old Mexico hand, or by the DPS in the White House, that it could have its cake and eat it too: a temporary workers' program without anything that even resembled amnesty, since Mexico would resignedly accept it, and the Republicans, with some help from a handful of conservative Democrats (now known as blue dogs), would get it approved in Congress. But it quickly became apparent to Colin Powell, at least, and to the technicians working on the issue, as well as to the political advisers in the White House, that the equation did not add up. The *political people* realized that the Republican right wing would not go along even with a TWP totally devoid of amnesty, and so they would inevitably require some Democratic votes, in the same way Bill Clinton only obtained passage for NAFTA thanks to moderate Republicans replacing left-wing Democrats. This point was made explicit in the spring of 2007 by House Speaker Nancy Pelosi in her negotiations with the White House: she would only provide Democratic votes in the House if Bush delivered at least thirty Republican members.

The *technicians* grasped that the first problem that had to be addressed was how to "marry" the undocumented already in the United States with the temporary workers who would come to the United States. And Powell understood that Fox and I would never go along with simply a guest-worker program, without meaningful concessions regarding the undocumented in the United States, because on principle we were not willing to forsake our compatriots abroad, or sell them down the river for a TWP, and in addition because we would be pilloried for doing it by Mexicans both south and north of the border.

A State Department document, dated September 7, 2001, and attributed to George Lannon and Steve Fischel, two Foggy Bottom "old hands," outlining talking points for Colin Powell, formulated the problem succinctly, when drawing up a series of generally agreed upon principles for regularization. They included the existence of incentives for various U.S. constituencies; its compatibility with Mexican political realities ("Fox cannot endorse a TWP without a comprehensive plan for dealing with undocumented Mexicans in the United States"); and its attractiveness to the undocumented themselves.* Each one of these desiderata were subsequently broken down into more detailed components. The same document stated that attractiveness to

---

*The full text of this paragraph reads as follows: "1) It (a Temporary Workers' Program) must be attractive to domestic constituencies: addressing a significant number of undocumented Mexicans resident in the United States, and provide some relief to those of other nationalities. 2) It must be attuned to Mexican political needs. Fox cannot endorse a TWP without a comprehensive plan for dealing with undocumented Mexicans in the United States. 3) It must be attractive to the undocumented: they will only come forward if provided a speedy and sure route to permanent residency; an undocumented restaurant employee with a family in Tucson would never risk his family's livelihood and future unless he was sure the program would not result in his deportation."

domestic constituencies entailed a plan that could reduce illegal immigration through cooperation by the source country, as well as incentives for workers to return home, and effective border enforcement by both countries. Being attractive to employers was defined as including a program that facilitated employer-employee matches; small businesses were unlikely to be able to find and hire the workers they needed in Mexico on their own, and would continue to rely on undocumented employees if not aided by the two governments. Moreover, the program needed to be significant in size: employers would have little incentive to participate if they expected a workforce mix of documented and undocumented to be disruptive and if undocumented aliens were continuously and immediately available for employment; thus, any functional program required a simple process for employer participation. And finally, any temporary-worker program had to serve Mexico's economic development; according to Powell's talking points, "the government of Mexico seeks a TWP that promotes circularity as a means of increasing remittances and providing work experience to its nationals. A worker residing in Mexico joins the TWP, works for a specified period of time in the United States and then returns permanently to Mexico."

Powell seems to have been persuaded that actually, Mexicans did not want to leave their country, and that providing them with partial, provisional but satisfactory alternatives was a good idea. In many discussions we tried to get this point across. Mexicans have for over a century come and gone north, and their first choice, their "best buy," their Plan A, is to do exactly that. And it is, by the way, a rational choice: to work hard half the year, often under highly adverse personal, professional, cultural, and even climatic circumstances, makes sense if one can spend the rest of the year back home, with the family, tending the plot, or the store, or just relaxing. Moreover, we also insisted, invariably and obsessively, that everything we were discussing and conceivably negotiating, was a bridge to another era. That era, which will probably begin around 2015, as almost every serious demographer appreciates, will usher in a new parameter in the immigration equation. The Mexican population is already aging rapidly, as fertility and birth rates have been dropping precipitously, and continue to plummet, for over twenty years now. By 2015, regardless of other circumstances, particularly economic ones, the pool of potential immigrants will have shrunk dramatically: only the young emigrate, and those over forty-five, a speedily growing share of Mexico's inhabitants, do not. Basically the point we tried to make with Powell and his aides in the State Department, and which I think they acknowledged, although their colleagues in the rest of the administration did not, was that if we legalized Mexicans in the United States, let others in to come and go, and waited out the fifteen years to 2015 (almost half of which has now already passed), the problem would be largely solved.*

---

*I confess I have begun to harbor some doubts about this aging demography thesis. Isaias Moreno—a childhood friend of mine from the Mexico City barrio of Actipan, where we grew up together—lost his job at the Veracruz Port Authority in 2004, did not find a new one, and, at the age of fifty-six, left for the United States. He first crossed in Tijuana, but was caught and thrown back, largely because his age, his girth, and more than four decades of fast and loose living had made climbing over the fence and then threading his way through the onrushing cars on I-5 impossible. He tried again, and almost died doing so, but he made it after walking through the mountains east of Tijuana for several days. He found a job at a Denny's coffee shop in San Diego making nearly $10 an hour with tips, until the apartment where he lived with friends was raided by ICE agents. He was shackled and deported, and went back to Veracruz; as he approaches sixty and greater despair than ever before, he may try again. It sounds absurd, but there is a logic to it: it is much more difficult to emigrate at that age, but it is also more difficult to find a local job at that age.

For all of these reasons, and particularly in view of the need to square the circle and include legalization and guest workers without saying so in so many words, the Bush administration decided to, as Powell eloquently put it, "bleed" the undocumented into legal status in the United States through the temporary-worker program, as certain textiles "bleed," particularly what used to be called Madras cloth when washed. The way they decided to solve the A-word dilemma was to disguise it as part of the guest worker arrangement, instead of calling it regularization—as we suggested—or legalization, as the liberals, Democrats, and Latinos called it. On substance, we were all referring to the same thing; every party wanted cover for reasons of political correctness, conviction, and convenience, but nobody could eliminate the substance. Either the issue was addressed, or it was not. In the same way the Mexican government attempted to finesse the question by changing the terminology, the U.S. administration sought to disguise the amnesty issue by folding it into the temporary-worker program; legalization would be accomplished by enrolling in the TWP, and eventually emerging from it through a path to residence and then citizenship.

This attempt first began at a meeting held on August 21, 2001, in El Paso, Texas. According to the notes taken by Gustavo Mohar and Rodolfo Tuirán, two exceptional Mexican senior officials present at the meeting, for the first time the American side explicitly stated that they were only authorized to propose the creation of a temporary-worker program, which, however, included an explicit component to regularize the immigration status of some undocumented Mexicans in the United States. But as the Mexicans reported back to their capital, "Despite their proposal, the American officials made it plain that they still did not have a clear idea of how that component would be incorporated into a Temporary Worker Program design."

In two State Department working papers dated August 2001, the American officials tried to define what they meant by a temporary-worker program. They took up, with a great deal of sensitivity and willingness to accommodate Mexico, almost all of the issues on the table, starting with "Why exclusively Mexico," to which they replied:

> While the United States has undocumented workers of many nationalities, Mexicans make up the majority. . . . Over the last century the United States has implemented several temporary-worker programs with Mexico. While all have failed for various reasons, there is, nonetheless, a history to build upon. Perhaps more importantly, Mexico is our neighbor. While we have extended special and unique immigration benefits to Canada, the United States has failed to extend similar privileges to Mexico. Therefore, singling out Mexico for this program demonstrates at least some recognition of special relationship between the two countries. . . .

They also tried to address all the other thorny questions. First, the selection process: Who chooses the workers? On the basis of what requirements or criteria? Who will choose the employers, and how? What are acceptable working conditions, and who will enforce them? What kind of control will there be on entry to the United States? Will the type of visa issued be portable, and for what interval between jobs? How long will the visa last? Will there be a (permanent) immigrant visa component? The authors of these documents were beginning to deal with the complications that would only become public several years later: the enormous challenge that had never been confronted in over a century of immigration relations between the two countries was the transition from migrants to immigrants;

as they said, "An immigrant program is essential in a temporary worker program."* From a purely substantive point of view, a temporary-worker program, as well as any guest-worker scheme, was not devoid of contradictions. Or, as a recent study by two World Bank economists phrased it: "Our results reveal that the use of Guest Worker schemes to compensate source countries for their cooperation (on illegal migration) is fraught with problems, and such a policy is not the first-best compared to, for example, monetary transfers" (Mohammed Amin and Aaditya Mattoo, "Can Guest Worker Schemes Reduce Illegal Migration?" World Bank Policy Research Working Paper 3828, February 2006). The authors essentially argue that source-country cooperation is indispensable to deter future illegal migration and to encourage or impose the return of already departed illegal migrants. In order to achieve that cooperation, they say, source countries need to obtain something from host countries, but guest-worker schemes are a less optimum compensation than direct monetary transfers from the host country to the source country. This reasoning, while probably accurate, is hardly applicable to Mexico and the United States, since no monetary compensation is even remotely conceivable on either side of the border. One reason for their skepticism is what they call the negative selection effect generated by guest-worker schemes: "If all agents have an equal chance of being selected for a GW

---

*"No previous guest-worker program with Mexico had an immigrant component. Such omission has contributed failure to these programs. History has revealed that one third of all guest workers become assimilated. Furthermore, workers in the US will need some motivation to come forward and enter the program. Knowing the program will last a designated period like three years, there is no incentive to 'regularize' if the reward for participation is undesired return to Mexico. So, an immigrant program is essential in a temporary worker program."

scheme, then such schemes involve negative selection, in that high-cost agents who would not migrate illegally get selected for legal migration. The benefit to source countries from substituting illegal with legal migration is therefore significantly eroded." Furthermore, they hold that "total migration (legal plus illegal) rises with the size of a GW scheme because such schemes induce the migration of high-cost agents who would otherwise not have migrated. Host countries that are primarily interested in controlling total migration, and are not concerned about its composition, will be made worse off by such schemes if they are implemented unilaterally." While these and other objections, particularly from the left—as we shall see in the following chapters—were neither inaccurate nor uninteresting, they begged the question of whether the ideal solution was politically viable, or whether what was politically viable was also acceptable, however imperfect.

This was the dilemma the Domestic Policy Council, and in general in the White House political operations center, refused to confront until 2006. On the one hand, in 2001, I believe they sincerely wanted an immigration agreement—because their boss wanted it—without paying too high a political cost; on the other, their technical and diplomatic advisers clearly explained that there was no such animal: no matter how much one tried to sweep the A-word under the rug, it came bouncing back. From late 2001 to mid-2005, the White House preferred to have no agreement nor comprehensive reform; then it concluded that it could have the best of both worlds, and disguise amnesty successfully: guest workers only, but with a path to permanent-immigrant status. That didn't work. Three years after the above-quoted documents were drafted, Bush's effort would turn out to be a very futile one: his own right-wing and comprehensive immigration reform's adversaries in the House of Representatives would denounce the bill approved by the Senate in June 2006 as amnesty in disguise, and would reject it on those grounds.

Nonetheless, as we shall see in the next chapters, both governments began to work on the issue indirectly, and separately, from thereon, or at least through early 2005, when, after Bush's reelection, they started talking again more or less seriously. Until then, the debate would shift to a different playing field: the U.S. congress and American civil society. But during those two years, both governments did part of their homework: Mexico by attempting to improve the lot of its nationals in the United States in the absence of any agreement and slowly assuming the practical, concrete consequences of shared responsibility; the United States in January 2004, when Bush decided to unilaterally propose a guest-worker program at a White House ceremony, evading the amnesty issue, though tacitly recognizing that it would have to be addressed somehow. We will return to these efforts in Chapter Seven; however, in Chapter Six, we will attempt to follow the shift to the other circles where the immigration discussion was playing out. We will also see how two new trends were emerging, as the numbers and dispersal of Mexicans across the United States were steeply rising. First, the conservative, nativist backlash against them was surging powerfully: in academia, with the publication of Samuel Huntington's *Who Are We? The Challenges to America's National Identity*; in public opinion, with polls showing that Americans' forebearance for immigration, illegal or not, was rapidly dropping; and in the Congress, where the anti-immigration caucus, led by people like Representative Tom Tancredo of Denver, Colorado, was expanding significantly. Second, proponents of immigration reform, tolerance, and cooperation were also gathering steam, and beginning to show their muscle.

SIX

In the spring of 2006, something happened to the Latino community in the United States. Suddenly, out of nowhere, hundreds of thousands—some said millions—of Mexicans, Salvadorans, Peruvians, Hondurans, Guatemalans, Colombians, Ecuadoreans, and Dominicans joined Puerto Ricans and Chicanos in dozens of public demonstrations all over the country. Some of the events took place where there had always been a large Hispanic agglomeration, except that it had remained in the shadows, surfacing only on Cinco de Mayo, Columbus Day, or the national independence holiday of each Latin nation: Chicago, Los Angeles, San Antonio, Houston. Others occurred where no one even knew there were so many Mexicans, or where they had never been sighted before: Atlanta, Phoenix, Detroit, Miami, Las Vegas, Denver, St. Paul, and San Diego, where, according to news accounts, between 50,000 and 100,000 demonstrators marched to central Balboa Park in one of most conservative, anti-immigrant cities in the United States. In the first round of marches, demonstrators carried their flags from their home countries: Mexican red and green, Salvadoran or Guatemalan blue and white, Dominican red and blue; in the next wave, after being censured for denationalizing their protests, the predominant colors in view were their new flags: white, for peace and amnesty, and the U.S. red, white, and blue. Some of the marches were linked to May Day celebrations and an economic show of force through job boycotting—A Day Without Mexicans; earlier in the spring, others were just protests and a show of pride, strength, and courage.

Who were the protesters? Who organized them? Many people asked these questions, bewildered at discovering what everyone in fact knew at least subconsciously. Literally millions of Mexicans and their neighbors from Central America, the Caribbean, and even South America now lived in the United States, in virtually every major city and many small towns, and they were part of everyone's lives. They washed dishes, mowed lawns, picked tomatoes, nurtured children, cleaned houses and offices, parked cars, and labored in sweatshops and at construction sites. They worked hard and long hours, paid their taxes in vain—to false Social Security accounts identified with false numbers and false cards, to the tune of $7 billion per year—and lived in the lonely, tough, and tragic circumstances so eloquently described by Jimmy Breslin in *The Short Sweet Dream of Eduardo Gutiérrez*. The Catholic Church helped organize the demonstrations, but so did local Spanish-language radio talk-show hosts, Hispanic television stations, service-worker unions, U.S. Latino groups and leaders, and, obviously, radical groups from the traditional American left, with their own causes, hopes, and slogans.

The Latino chants were crisp and smart: "Today we march, tomorrow we vote" and "We didn't cross the border; the border crossed us"; the marches were all peaceful and tightly run, without incidents; many elected Chicano officials, including Los Angeles Mayor Antonio Villaraigosa, supported them or participated, proclaiming, "Today we say to America, we've come here to work. We clean your toilets. We clean your hotels. We build your houses. We take care of your children. We want you to help us take care of our children as well." Obviously many of the protesters were in the United States without papers; those with papers had much less to protest about and were in fact only showing solidarity with a cause that was alien to them directly, but dear to them emotionally. According to one calculation by a group of researchers from the Woodrow Wilson International Center for Scholars in Washington, from 3.5 to 5 million people participated in the marches that took place over a couple of months in more than twenty cities: an astonishing number given the specificity of their motivations. Indeed, in some cities, like Los Angeles, Phoenix, Chicago, Dallas, Fresno, and San Jose, according to this study ("Invisible No More: Mexican Migrant Civic Participation in the United States"), these were the largest mobilizations ever in these communities, including the civil rights movements, the Vietnam War protests, and Iraq.

The demonstrations were largely directed against something, and only vaguely in favor of an alternative. What brought the hidden and frightened into the sun was the Border Protection, Anti-Terrorism and Illegal Immigration Control Act, approved by the House of Representatives in December 2005. Instead of providing for the kind of real and realistic immigration reform that Fox, Bush, Democrats, and moderate Republicans had hoped for, it sought the opposite: to criminalize illegal entry into the United States, making it a felony punishable by one year imprisonment, instead of a misdemeanor; to build a seven-hundred-mile fence along the Mexican border; to severely punish employers who hired unauthorized workers and those citizens who gave support, sanctuary, or any aid to "illegal aliens." It also contained many other hateful provisions, including granting state and local law enforcement authorities the right to investigate, identify, arrest, or transfer to federal custody "aliens" for the purpose of enforcing immigration laws; it facilitated and hastened the deportation of "illegals," establishing mandatory deportation and denial of immigration status to asylum seekers, workers, and others for doing what they needed to survive in the United States. It was traditional American nativism transformed into law.

Known as the Sensenbrenner Bill, after the ultra-conservative Republican chairman of the House Judiciary Committee, it incensed the Catholic Church (Roger Cardinal Mahoney of Los Angeles was particularly furious, since many priests in his and other Catholic dioceses indeed provided sanctuary to "illegals"), Democrats (Hillary Clinton called it an ungodly act), the AFL-CIO, and even President Bush. Some observers sought to minimize the demonstrations, using arguments that, while not entirely false, were insufficient to explain the extraordinary outpouring of people, sentiment, and courage. It was true that many of those who marched were either permanent residents already, protesting more in solidarity with their friends or relatives in the shadows than on behalf of their own interests. Many other participants were clearly Latinos, in the strict definition of the term: American citizens of Hispanic descent, who were acting in the name of others. And finally, it was also true that because unauthorized migrants would be the main victims of the Sensenbrenner Bill—if it ever passed the Senate and Bush signed it—they had little to lose by marching against it. The worst that could happen to them—be detained and deported for protesting against the bill—was exactly what in their minds would occur if the bill were passed.

On previous occasions it had been proved that migrants in the shadows react very rapidly and drastically to news accounts of changes in their situations; given the stridency of the Spanish-language media in broadcasting the news, and since their audiences tend to take them somewhat literally, many migrants thought that they would be literally deported the day after the bill was passed by the House. But none of these arguments can alter the fact that the unauthorized migrants—whatever the number they represented in the total of demonstrators, and regardless of their specific motivations—showed enormous courage and discipline. They risked arrest, deportation, and loss of jobs and day wages; they were denounced and ostracized by those who forgot that many of the labor movement conquests in the United States at the turn of the twentieth century were achieved by foreigners striking and marching in the streets; they were accused of everything from being traitors and ungrateful to opportunistic and "fifth columnists"; yet they held firm. On occasion groups from the traditional U.S. left—from the extreme fringe to the AFL-CIO—tried to manipulate them; it generally didn't work.

They went out and marched, and achieved victory in their short-term objectives. The Sensenbrenner Bill would never become law, because there were sufficient Senate (Democratic and Republican) votes to filibuster it to death. This might have been the outcome even without the marches, but the marches made a huge difference. Many moderate Republicans, beginning with Arizona Senator John McCain, realized that their party could not afford to permanently alienate the Hispanic vote, and that the intricacies of Latino politics—who is a Mexican unauthorized worker, who is a permanent resident eligible for citizenship, who is a citizen eligible to vote, who is a registered voter, who is a Democrat, and what are the relations between each one of these different realities of Latino identity in the United States—were too complex to be managed through simplistic right-wing posturing and grandstanding. The moderate Republicans were right: in the November 2006 midterm elections, the Hispanic vote rose to more than 8 percent of the electorate, and seven of every ten Latinos voted for Democrats, erasing the recent and minor but promising inroads that Bush and Karl Rove had made into the Hispanic electorate in 2000 and 2004.

In fact, the mass demonstrations and amazing awakening of the migrant, undocumented, and largely Mexican population left unanswered two traditional questions, one in the United States, one in Mexico. Would the street protesters eventually be voters? Would those who were already U.S. citizens begin to exercise their right to vote in higher percentages, and would they continue to do so with a very strong Democratic bias? Would the Mexicans or Central Americans among them eventually become legal permanent residents, and subsequently U.S. citizens, and then high-turnout voters? The evidence from IRCA in the 1980s would seem to suggest an affirmative answer to the latter set of questions, and growing voter participation by Latinos in California in particular hints at an equally affirmative response to the former query. But the jury is still out, and the first real trial—the 2008 U.S. presidential elections— may not prove conclusive. The two candidates could both turn out to be attractive to Hispanic voters—for example, Clinton and Giuliani or Obama and McCain—and it may be too soon for any significant expansion in the Latino electorate to have occurred. Still, if past indications hold about how mass activism in the streets and campuses eventually feeds into the electoral process in the United States, then one day soon the slogan will become true: "Today we march, tomorrow we vote."

The protests also unleashed a series of questions in and around Mexico. As Jorge Bustamante has lamented, Mexicans in Mexico by and large paid little heed to the demonstrations. There were few if any solidarity marches; practically no organizations in Mexico sent donations to the groups in the United States; the Mexican Congress, which normally expresses its support or opinions regarding just about anything that occurs in the world, was remarkably silent. Bustamante has attributed this long-standing indifference—which, as we saw in earlier chapters, has evolved in recent years—to what he calls the "atavistic and closeted racism of Mexican society" toward migrants. At the end of the day, Mexicans still apparently feel that once a migrant crosses the border, he or she enters a different world for which they have no sympathy or empathy, no matter how much they depend on it for remittances, social stability, and access to modernity. Certainly the distance in relation to the marches was perplexing, and Bustamante's explanation rings true.

Several converging trends had brought the issue back to the front-burner in 2004, mainly after that year's presidential elections. In order of importance they were, as I already described, the linkage of immigration issues to security considerations; the growing magnitude of the immigration phenomenon itself and the issue's intrinsic merits and substance; Bush's commitment—oscillating and wavering as it may have been—to the matter; and, to a lesser degree, the Mexican government's insistence, less after 9/11, much less during 2003 and 2004, to getting something done. Fox had paid a high price for thinking—and verbalizing his conviction—that he could get a deal on migration from Bush; his opponents reveled in highlighting his failure and Bush's "hypocrisy." Americans who, for reasons implicating their own agenda, had always considered the immigration issue to be a minor one or at best a nonstarter also fell into an "I told you so" mood with the Mexicans, without of course ever confessing where they stood: in favor of an immigration agreement or not. After the falling-out with Bush on Iraq, there was little Fox could do to push forward his immigration agenda, other than keep bringing it up each time he met with Bush or spoke with him on the phone. Bush, for his part, kept repeating that he would not abandon the issue, that he would return to it—as he did with his speech in January 2004 calling for a guest-worker program, as we shall see further ahead—and also explaining to Fox that the best way to go about reaching their common destination was for something to emerge from Congress itself, and in particular from the Senate. What sprang forth from the Senate, much later, in mid-2005, was the most important piece of immigration legislation to surface since IRCA in 1986, and came to be known as the McCain-Kennedy Bill on immigration reform. Its formal name was the Secure America and Orderly Immigration Act; it was introduced in the U.S. Senate in May 2005 and in the House by Representatives Luis Gutiérrez from Chicago and Jim Kolbe from Arizona. Many factors contributed to its materialization, and they are worth examining in some detail.

The first factor that contributed to the emergence of the McCain-Kennedy piece of legislation was, of course, the sheer growth in the dimensions of the immigration question. As we already saw, because of the collapse of circularity (the restoration of which was explicitly mentioned in the McCain-Kennedy Bill), there were far more Mexicans than ever in the United States, and far more immigrants from other nations also. The total foreign-born population—legal or otherwise—grew 16 percent from 2000 to 2005, rising from 30.8 million to 35.7 million, and expanding from 11.2 percent to 12.4 percent of the total U.S. population; these figures were calculated by the U.S. Bureau of the Census on a household basis, excluding prison, hospital, and university occupants. The highest historical percentage of the foreign-born population in the United States reached 14.8 percent in 1890, slightly above the 14.4 percent for 1870, a tiny bit above the 14.7 percent for 1910. It then declined, decreasing to its lowest point ever, 4.7 percent in 1970, then beginning to rise again, from 6.2 percent in 1980 to 7.9 percent in 1990 and 11.1 percent in 2000, the highest share in the decennial census since 11.6 percent in 1930. The 12.4 percent for 2006 was the highest proportion since the mid-1920s, and may in fact be higher, since there is probably some undercounting, given the large number of undocumented foreign-born. In any case, as *The New Americans: A Guide to Immigration since 1965* reported in 2006, "between 2000 and 2005, an estimated 7.9 million immigrants arrived, the largest number arriving in a five-year period in the nation's history."

The *Mexican-born* population grew faster than the overall foreign cohort, at a rate of 20.7 percent, rising from 9.1 to 11 million. The Mexican *undocumented* population, insofar as the available figures are accurate indicators, also increased, from 3.5 to 6.7 million: almost doubling, and expanding much more rapidly than the foreign-born and the overall undocumented, which went from 8.4 to 11.7 million in 2005, an increase of nearly 30 percent. Again, this meant more Mexicans in more places than ever before, even if the yearly arrivals held more or less steady, at around 400,000. The problems increased, the backlash intensified, and the need to do something gained traction in Washington, as Bush procrastinated on the issue, and some Democrats realized there was political mileage to be obtained from it. This was particularly true after the 2004 elections, which they lost across the board, while at the same time the Latino vote was becoming increasingly crucial: witness the election of Antonio Villaraigosa as mayor of Los Angeles, the first Latino mayor in modern times of the world's second-largest "Mexican City." Something had to be done.

The odious Sensenbrenner Bill was indeed an ideological product of nativist backlash, directed against the rise and diffusion of migrants everywhere in the United States. But it was also the conservative Republican, legislative response to the McCain-Kennedy proposal. Senators John McCain and Edward Kennedy had been working for months on an immigration reform bill. By the time their final product materialized, the basic parameters of the equation, essentially fleshed out during the 2001 talks between the two governments, were clear to just about everybody. The conundrums that had emerged back in 2001 had all their facets reexamined in 2005 and 2006. The questions and the answers that had to be confronted in 2005–6 with McCain-Kennedy, and then subsequently in the Senate Judiciary Committee, turned out to be essentially the same ones the two governments grappled with in 2001–2, and the same ones addressed by the modified and watered-down bill that was approved by the full Senate in May 2006, known as the Comprehensive Immigration Reform Act. They were also remarkably similar to more recent bipartisan, sensible proposals, such as the Spencer Abraham/Lee Hamilton Migration Policy Institute Task Force Report, issued in late 2006.

Like the discussions that took place between the governments of Mexico and the United States in 2001 and 2002, the Senate attempt to deal with immigration contemplated the multiple facets of the issue, and two in particular: the status of unauthorized persons already in the United States, and a guest-worker program for future entries. The first and most novel ingredient of importance in the McCain-Kennedy initial "considering" paragraphs lay in the fact that they explicitly linked immigration with U.S. national security: "The United States cannot effectively carry out its national security policies unless the United States identifies undocumented immigrants and encourages them to come forward and participate legally in the economy of the United States. . . ." The McCain-Kennedy Bill also euphemistically addressed cooperation with Mexico: "Foreign governments, particularly those that share an international border with the United States, must play a critical role in securing international borders and deterring illegal entry of foreign nationals into the United States."

Again, the reality of the security-immigration link was much less evident than its politics. Senators Kennedy and McCain, as well as the other Democrats and moderate Republicans who pushed the bill forward, realized, along with President Bush, that it was much easier to sell immigration reform bundled together with security considerations than separately. The question of course was: sell to whom? The Republican right wing would never buy into anything that smacked of amnesty; the Republican moderates did not really need the cover, although it was useful; and American public opinion did not seem to establish any sort of link whatsoever, if the myriad polls taken during the spring and summer of 2006 were any indication. And five years' experience since 9/11 did not suggest any linkage: there had been no public evidence at all of anyone caught crossing into the United States from Mexico with terrorist connections; and no proof of any terrorist ties or activities in Mexican neighborhoods, new or old, had been unearthed.

If anything, there were growing suggestions that part of the overall decrease in crime in the United States, and, in certain big cities, had to do with the explosion in the Mexican immigrant population: Mexicans were less prone to crime because of the strength of the Mexican family, because of the need to keep out of trouble given their vulnerability, and because of the obsession to work more hours in order to send more money home. Were someone to calculate the personal savings rate of Mexican undocumented workers in the United States, it would reach Asian heights; and high savers do not commit crimes or plant bombs. And Americans seemed to acknowledge this. When they were asked in a poll carried out in February 2003 by Zogby International if they agreed or not with the statement that immigrants are more likely than American-born citizens to commit crimes, 37.38 percent strongly disagreed while only 11.5 percent said they strongly agreed; more recently, in a similar poll carried out by Associated Press and Ipsos in May 2006, 19 percent of Americans thought immigrants were more likely to be involved in criminal activity than people born in the United States while 12 percent said they were less likely and 68 percent considered there was not much difference.

Two academic studies produced the same results. Robert Sampson from Harvard, along with Jeffrey Morenoff of the University of Michigan and Stephen Raudenbush from the University of Chicago, studied 3,000 young inhabitants from Chicago from 1995 to 2002, a large number of which were first- or second-generation immigrants. They found that "a person's immigrant status emerged as a stronger indicator of a dispropensity to violence than any other factor. First-generation immigrants are 45 percent less likely to commit violence than third-generation immigrants. Mexican Americans were the least violent." Sampson summarized his conclusions in an op-ed piece published in the *New York Times* in March 2006 in which he explained why this was so: fear of deportation, living with married adults, conservative opinions on drugs and crime, etc. He even suggested that the drop of criminality detected in large cities over the past decade might be attributable to the spike in immigration. Another report, drawn up by Ruben Rumbaut and Walter Ewing for the American Immigration Law Foundation and the Immigration Policy Center and issued in February 2007, corroborated these findings. Although the undocumented population doubled between 1994 and 2006, the violent crime rate in the United States declined 34 percent. Among men aged between eighteen and thirty-nine, the incarceration rate of the native-born was five times higher than among the foreign-born. Foreign-born Mexicans had an incarceration rate eight times lower than the rate of native-born males of Mexican descent. Conversely, second- and third-generation immigrants "become subject to economic and social forces, such as the higher rates of family disintegration and drug and alcohol addiction, that increase the likelihood of criminal behavior among natives."

The McCain-Kennedy legislative proposal established new rules for hiring foreign temporary workers through an H5A Essential Worker Visa Program, accepting at least 400,000 workers each year, their visas lasting three years with one renewal if they had a job in the United States, paid a $500 fee, and cleared security and medical checks. At the end of the visa period, the worker either had to return home or be in the pipeline for a green card; the visa was considered portable from job to job, but only with a two-month interval between positions. In very explicit terms, McCain-Kennedy established the bilateral nature of its approach: the law would have required foreign countries to enter into "migration agreements with the United States that help control the flow of their citizens to jobs in the United States," with emphasis on encouraging "circularity," that is, the reintegration of their citizens as they returned home. It also contemplated what it called partnership with Mexico to promote economic opportunity back home and reduce the pressure to immigrate.

The proposed law equally provided for conditional legalization of undocumented migrants in the United States. The latter would have to register with the new INS or Immigration and Customs Enforcement (ICE), pay a $2,000 fine, clear a criminal-background check, and pass an English exam; if they had a standing job, they could remain legally in the United States and apply for citizenship six years later. In other words, there was both a legalization provision and a path to residence and citizenship: exactly what Powell and I had wanted, what Bush had reluctantly accepted without pushing for it, and what the Republican right wing abhorred. The McCain-Kennedy Bill sought to increase fines for employers hiring "illegals" and strengthen border security, while expanding the number of green cards or permanent resident status holders, reducing the huge existing backlog of people waiting in line—more than 750,000 Mexicans.

This sensible bipartisan bill enraged the anti-amnesty conservative caucus, which had grown from a few Republican congressmen at the turn of the century, led by extremists like Tom Tancredo from Colorado, to more than one hundred members who introduced the Sensenbrenner Bill, starting with Wisconsin representative James Sensenbrenner himself. It infuriated them because it was the first piece of legislation to actually be presented on immigration since the entire process began in 2001; because it had prestigious bipartisan support; because it addressed the indispensable series of ingredients any immigration reform needed—stock and flow, past and future, legalization and guest workers— and because it explicitly entailed Mexican cooperation. In other words, the Republican right wing opposed it because it made sense and because it could succeed. But they also rejected it vehemently for another reason: their constituents were "mad as hell" about "illegal immigration" and they were not going to take it.

Indeed, the rabid opposition awakened by McCain-Kennedy sprung from the entire process I have already described, and which was beginning to "bite" in the heartland. It was the wrong reaction to a misunderstood challenge brought about by mistaken policies with unintended effects. But it was neither a totally unexpected nor unpredictable response to that challenge. The breakdown of circularity represented a massive dose of growth hormone to the stock of undocumented immigrants, Latino workers, and, very specifically, Mexican migrants. The ensuing spike in the numbers generated the completely logical consequence of diffusion: Mexicans finding jobs, settling, and bringing their families to join them in places where Spanish had never been spoken, chiles and tortillas were never eaten, mariachi and *grupera* music were never heard, and a Catholic church with Sunday mass was as alien as a minaret or a Buddhist stupa. And this diffusion, in turn, provoked a traditional and understandable, however inexcusable, backlash: throw them out or in jail, shut the doors and windows, pillory and denounce them. Part of the backlash was simple, downright racist nativism; part was academic rejection of new phenomena and uncharted waters; part was political grandstanding by right-wing Republicans and strident television anchors who thought there were ratings and votes to be conquered this way. The representatives in the U.S. Congress of these confused, exacerbated, and often uncontrollable sentiments thought they had stopped immigration reform, amnesty, and anything associated with it after 9/11; they thought they had weaned George Bush from his Mexican temptation or softness; they were sure they had sent Fox packing; when suddenly, a bill jointly submitted by one of

their champions, John McCain, and one of their bêtes noires—
or the devil himself—Ted Kennedy, attempted to turn things
around.

Their reaction was rational, insofar as rationality in these
matters exists at all: they were not going to allow it. One cannot sympathize with these views, but one can certainly understand where they come from, and why they surged forth across
the United States when they did. A few numbers on the composition of the Mexican-born workforce in the United States
cast some light on where and why. According to a November
2006 study by the Migration Policy Institute, based on that
year's Current Population Survey, it accounted for one-third of
the foreign-born workforce and 5 percent of the total civilian
labor force. Males made up 70 percent of the total, in contrast
to the 60 percent male composition of the entire foreign-born
working population, and the 52 percent male share of the native workforce. The Mexican labor cohort was much younger
than everyone else: 77 percent were under forty-five, whereas
66 percent of the entire foreign-born workforce and 59 percent
of native workers were below that age. Most significantly, perhaps, for opponents of immigration from Mexico, 60 percent had
not completed high school, while 28 percent of the foreign-
born total hadn't, and only 6.5 percent of the native labor force
did not have a high-school education. So the Mexican labor
force was growing, younger, and less educated than anyone else
and, in addition, concentrated in low-skill jobs like construction as well as leisure and hospitality (almost 40 percent of the
total). It might not yet be a permanent underclass, but it certainly was beginning to reflect the typical composition of one.
Worse still, because of its youth, low educational level, and
male component, it seemed destined to grow, as women came

to join their companions, as they had babies, and as the babies became—inevitably—underprivileged American citizens.

An example of these facts' translations into everyday life in certain regions of the United States emerged in Louisiana, slightly more than a year after Hurricane Katrina. There had never been many Mexicans in the New Orleans metropolitan area, although in the 1990s some showed up to work in the oil industry in southern Louisiana, as Katherine M. Donato, Melissa Stainback, and Carl L. Bankston III show in *New Destinations*. There were so few that in 2002, when the Mexican Foreign Ministry carried out a minor reorganization of our consulates abroad, opening new ones where there were recent Mexican settlements and closing others where there were none, we shut down the one in New Orleans. That year, the consulate in New Orleans delivered 1,297 consular IDs, one of the lowest totals in the nation. It's only raison d'être was that nineteenth-century Mexican president and "father of the fatherland" Benito Juárez had lived in New Orleans, and subsequently established Mexico's first consulate there. We decided to open up a new substitute office for the entire region, located either in Memphis or Little Rock; my successor picked—wisely, I think—the capital of Arkansas in view of the burgeoning number of Mexicans toiling in the Tyson poultry plants.

But when Hurricane Katrina hit and destroyed a good part of the city, a good part of it had to be rebuilt. And literally droves of Latinos, from as far away as Honduras and as close by as Houston and Beaumont across the state line in Texas, rushed to participate in the reconstruction effort and business. Again, as always, most of them were Mexicans, drifting in from other locations in the United States: North Carolina, Georgia (where many had begun to find construction jobs since the Atlanta

Olympic Games), Florida, and the Midwest. In 2006, five thousand consular IDs were handed out in New Orleans by a reopened consulate: four times the number for 2002. As the *New York Times* reported slightly more than a year after Katrina, a "baby boom" occurred: a sixfold Latino adult population explosion that reached, according to some estimates, nearly 60,000 Hispanics—in a city whose overall population was shrinking by the day. This led to another explosion: births of American citizens, born of the hard days' nights in flooded parishes of the Mississippi Delta, to thousands of undocumented Mexicans. Mothers strained emergency wards in local hospitals, clinics, and welfare centers; risked their lives and that of their offspring because of the hardship under which they labored and were in labor; and created a new Mexican settlement behind the rebuilt levees. A few years from now, the numbers will show that the largely African American Big Easy will rapidly become the Latina "Gran Tranquila": Benito Juárez would be proud.

Given these evolving realities, it was not exactly surprising that American nativism would rear its ugly head or that it would be reflected in legislative, academic, and public opinion circles. Despite all the hyperbole on talk radio and cable television, most polls showed that Americans were of mixed minds about immigration itself, reforming it, and regarding what to do about it. Polling numbers on immigration issues are particularly sensitive to exactly how a given question is asked or phrased, but in general terms the United States seemed roughly split in half on immigration. According to an Associated Press/Ipsos poll taken in May 2006, more or less the same proportion (52 percent versus 46 percent) of Americans considered immigrants a good or bad influence on the way things were going in the United States. The same proportion was in favor of more or less immigration. It was likewise with deporting or legalizing those who were already in the country without papers: 67 percent were for deportation, according to a June 2006 CNN poll, versus 77 percent for legalization in a May 2006 CBS poll; 51 percent were in favor of a guest-worker program and 27 percent were against in a June 2006 *Los Angeles Times* poll, and similar percentages believed migrants took jobs Americans did not want at all or at the wages foreigners accepted versus those who believed they took jobs away from Americans. Finally, the same Associated Press/Ipsos poll quoted above showed that 22 percent of Americans thought that immigrants improved their community, while 18 percent believed they created problems, and 58 percent thought they had not much effect on their communities.

Obviously, many of the responses were understandably contradictory, given the complexity of the issue: against deportation, but also against amnesty; against more immigration, but also opposing a wall or a system seeking to close the border (29 percent in favor, 66 percent against, in a May 2006 CBS/New York Times poll); accepting that migrants contribute to the U.S. economy, but not wanting more of them. All of which meant two things: this was not an issue any party could make political hay of. The Democrats could consolidate their traditional share of the growing volume of the Latino vote, but not much more; Republicans would not succeed in transforming the matter into a traditional wedge issue, like gay marriage, stem-cell research, or even abortion. Second, politicians would have to lead on the issue: public opinion would not automatically drive them in one direction or another.

Academically, the main tacit response to the approach behind McCain-Kennedy and the Bush and Fox attempts to kick the can down the road was Professor Samuel Huntington's controversial—for some racist and for others on-the-money—

Who Are We? The Challenges to America's National Identity. In the chapters dedicated to Hispanic, and particularly Mexican, immigration to the United States, the legendary Harvard professor argued that the Mexican exodus was different from others for several reasons. One was Mexico's contiguity to the United States. The others were the scale of its migratory flow, its illegal nature, its concentration within certain states in the southwestern United States, its persistence over time, the potency and omnipresence of the Spanish language, and, finally, its history. One could argue with many of the details in Huntington's text, and many of his statistics lacked precision or were questionable and obsolete, or, as in the case of the concentration in certain states, had become so. But some of the fundamental trends he described were partly true, and therefore some of his points were partly valid: Mexican immigrants are not being assimilated into the American melting pot the way other ethnic groups have been in the past. I have described at length why this has been so, at least through the era of circularity: Mexicans come and go, could live as Mexicans in the United States, with their own language, religion, movies, music, television, newspapers, food, and sports, and at the same time keep the family back home, with all their rights and perks intact. Indeed, by some calculations, the overall Mexican economy in the United States is almost the exact same size as the Mexican economy.

Many Americans intuitively sense this state of affairs, which makes scholars like Huntington nervous; perhaps he was just refining their perceptions. According to an NPR/Kaiser/Kennedy School poll conducted in mid-2004, 64 percent of nonimmigrants believe the United States "is a country made up of many cultures and values that change as people come here," while only 34 percent considered the United States to be a country with a basic American culture and values that immigrants take on when they come here. *But 62 percent thought the United States should be the latter, while only 33 percent thought it should be the former.*

Huntington believes this situation will condemn Mexicans in the United States to the status of a permanent, separate minority, in perpetual confrontation with the majority, something that few people in Mexico consider desirable for Mexico, and that few people in the United States consider desirable for the United States. The most serious defect in Huntington's theory, however, was that he characterized this situation as undesirable but offered no solution to the problems that created it, thereby allowing his argument to be manipulated by racist or nativist advocates, which Huntington is not. He is a conservative, not a racist. The Mexican experience *is* different from that of other immigrant groups in the past: assimilation *is not* automatic or spontaneous. Mexicans, for example, have only recently begun to acquire U.S. citizenship in significant numbers. This is partly due to IRCA and the waiting period it established after amnesty in 1986; it is partly the result of the 1996 immigration scare unleashed by the Clinton administration, which led many Mexican permanent residents to seek naturalization out of a possibly unwarranted but undeniable fear of losing their status; and it is partly because of the 1998 double-nationality law promulgated in Mexico by Ernesto Zedillo, mentioned in Chapter One. For years the number of Mexicans obtaining U.S. citizenship was abysmally low, and Huntington's argument was partly borne out by this fact. During the 1960s, the annual figure ranged from 5,000 to 7,000 per year, around 5 percent of all naturalizations; in the following decade, the yearly average was approximately 6,000 again, and in the 1980s it ranged from 8,000 to 14,000. After 1984, it began to rise sharply, without ever reaching 10 percent of the total.

But by 1996, the figure jumped to 254,607, that is, almost a fourth of the total, and far more than countries like China, Vietnam, the Philippines, or India. It is true that with the exception of 1999, the first year after Mexico allowed dual citizenship, when it crept back up to 207,072, the total began declining again: from 189,051 in 2000 to 102,736 in 2001, 76,310 in 2002, and 55,946 in 2003. Then it inched upward again in 2004 to 63,840, and rose again a bit in 2005 to 77,089. It is likely that the upswing during these last two years will become a permanent trend, although this is not yet evident.

Many factors explain this overall, relative Mexican exceptionality, foremost among them contiguity and continuity, as many experts and even I argued as early as 1987, in my *Limits to Friendship* (with Robert Pastor); rarely has a migratory current lasted as long as the Mexican one to the United States, and rarely has the distance been so short, from point of departure to point of arrival, making circularity *physically* easier than elsewhere. The language barrier is also partly responsible, as are a first-generation lower educational level and discrimination. Although past waves of immigrants to the United States, including the Irish, Poles, Italians, and Jews, were victims of racism and exclusion, the case can be made that Mexicans suffer from a more acute form of bias than those other groups did. Because Mexican immigration has created a new and different situation, the United States must construct a new and different type of assimilation model for Hispanics—one that is explicit and voluntary. I shall return to the assimilation debate in the concluding chapter; for now, suffice it to say that building a new model should not be that difficult. Despite all the brouhaha and conventional wisdom about Mexican anti-Americanism, the above-quoted NPR/Kaiser/Kennedy School poll showed that Mexican immigrants (i.e., permanent legal residents or naturalized citizens), compared to Central or South American immigrants, had a better opinion of the United States than of their own country, or than all other immigrants. With regard to opportunities to get ahead, the difference between Mexicans and others was 14 percent (94 percent versus 80 percent); on women's legal rights, 18 percent (83 percent versus 65 percent); on treatment of the poor, 22 percent (76 percent versus 54 percent); regarding schools, 25 percent (63 percent versus 38 percent); even on moral values of society, perhaps a more cultural question, 14 percent, though with a relatively dim view of the United States (38 percent versus 24 percent). The only issue on which Mexicans, Central and South Americans, and all other immigrants thought the same, and on which the United States fared poorly when compared to their own countries, was "Relations between races/ethnic groups": only 38 percent, 32 percent, and 38 percent, respectively, thought the United States was better than their own countries in this regard.

In the U.S. Congress, as legislation worked its way through the process, the Republican conservatives were able to throw several monkey wrenches into the McCain-Kennedy machinery, largely as result of Bush's lackadaisical attitude and reticence to spend political capital on the issue. The Democrats in the Senate, mainly Kennedy, then minority leader Harry Reid, Dianne Feinstein, David Durbin, and a few others, together with their sensible Republican colleagues—McCain, Richard Lugar, Chuck Hagel, Mel Martínez, and a couple more—obviously in agreement, not to say connivance, with the White House and Karl Rove, thought they could get sufficient votes in the Senate to stop a filibuster and sufficient votes to pass in the House if they watered down McCain-Kennedy sufficiently. They were wrong, and this was one additional miscalculation in the entire immigration drama of the last five years. Kennedy and McCain, encouraged by a White House promising things it could not deliver at the end of the day, accepted a series of concessions—some understandable, others incomprehensible and utterly impractical—in order to obtain enough Senate votes, which they got, and the necessary House votes, which they did not. They sharply reduced the number of new permanent visas, and the scope of the guest-worker program, down to 250,000 per year, thus creating the conditions that encourage more undocumented flows: not everybody fits. Then, most absurdly, they established a sort of turnstile or so-called touchback arrangement, whereby Mexicans in the United States were divided into three tiers: those who had been in the United States more than six years, those who arrived between two and six years ago, and those who had less than two years under their belt. The first batch could apply directly for residence and achieve it if its members qualified; the third group had to go home (they never will, of course, and the cost of finding and deporting them is exorbitant); but the second cohort had to travel to an authorized border crossing point (apparently nineteen were approved), leave the United States, and return hours later with a visa that would eventually allow them to be transferred into the first batch. But in addition to the obvious question—why make things so complicated and provide new and better business for the coyotes?—the more painful and hateful aspects of this approach were rapidly exposed: what would happen to a family in which the father belonged to the first group, the mother to the second one, and the Mexican-born children to the third one; or in which the mother of American-born children belonged to the third one?

In any case, the Senate-approved bill did not move forward in the House, which approved a seven-hundred-mile fence or wall on the U.S.-Mexican border—a highly offensive decision for Mexico, and one rejected by most Americans, according to polls—which also died once the Democrats won back majorities in the House and Senate in November 2006.

During this debate others tried to bridge the differences and finesse both the amnesty issue and the temporary-worker dilemma. This was the case of the bipartisan report from the Independent Task Force on Immigration and America's Future, chaired by Spencer Abraham, Bush's first secretary of energy, and Lee Hamilton, a long-term Democratic congressman from Indiana and former chairman of the House Foreign Affairs Committee.

The group tried to establish differences through other approaches—particularly distancing itself from the wording of a previous guest-worker program—but its stance on temporary workers and amnesty sounded pretty much the same as what had been said since 2001. It preferred three types of visas: temporary, provisional, and permanent. The first category "would be issued for short-term stays and work assignments, such as seasonal employment." The second type of visa "would allow employers to recruit foreign-born workers for permanent jobs and possible future immigration after a testing period of several years"; and the third type—the permanent kind—would "be available both to those who apply directly and those who 'graduate' from provisional status." The report was very specific in the conditions it was proposing for this approach: "Any strategy to reduce illegal immigration must . . . increase the numbers of workers admitted legally"; "temporary and provisional workers should have the right to change employers after an initial period without jeopardizing their immigration status, and to exercise labor rights comparable to those of similarly employed U.S. workers." On the most controversial question, the one creating the most problems and affecting, for now, the largest number of people, the report was unambiguous: "An earned path to permanent legal status is the most urgent immigrant integration need at this time."* It insisted that standards for legalization should be the same for everybody, and that it should occur as part of comprehensive immigration reform.

By the end of 2006, it was clear that the stage was set in the U.S. Congress, and in American society in general. What had been proposed five years before seemed increasingly feasible, and at least partly accepted by the American electorate in the November elections of last year. The new Democratic majorities in the House and Senate, together with Bush, McCain, and other moderate (on this issue) Republicans appeared to be forging a de facto coalition for comprehensive immigration reform that also implied an agreement with Mexico. This was the result of all the converging and contradictory processes we have seen here, but also the product of the two governments' work. We must now turn to that.

---

*The report said: "The requirements for earning legal status should be the same for all eligible applicants. A legalization process should be simple, with an eligibility date that is as recent as possible. The process should include registration for work eligibility in the United States, accompanied by a background security check, English-language requirements, and payment of a substantial fine for illegally entering the United States. Earned legal status should occur within the context of broad, comprehensive immigration reform."

SEVEN

The Mexican government reacted—as swiftly as possible, in my opinion, belatedly in that of its critics—to the shift in U.S. opinion and climate brought about by September 11th. We already examined the substance of the adjustment, but that was perhaps not the most important response. The main one involved the decision the authorities took to address the everyday concerns of millions of undocumented Mexicans in the United States, concerns that hopefully would be dealt with through a migration agreement but that in the meantime required imaginative action. That principal decision, already in the works before 9/11, entailed overhauling the Mexican Consular Identification Card, and handing it out on a massive scale to Mexican nationals in the United States. The process began in late 2001.

Mexico's successive governments had been delivering IDs for decades, but they were largely worthless, partly because the requirements for obtaining one were almost nonexistent, partly because they were extremely easy to forge, and partly because no one in the United States took them seriously. They were useful to individuals from south of the border mainly as proof of citizenship on reentering Mexico, in the long-gone era of circularity. Serendipity happens, though: the automatic photo and printing devices purchased from Polaroid for every Mexican consulate years before had gotten old, and Polaroid had gone out of business. When searching for a substitute, my deputy in charge of North American affairs—Ambassador Enrique Berruga, whom George W. Bush always referred to as the "water man," since he handled Mexico's Rio Grande Valley water debt and negotiations—suggested we set up a new system. It would include a more serious document-verification procedure and nine security checks to prevent forgery. The new ID was more authentic and more secure and looked the part. It is true, as many conservatives in the United States subsequently argued, that Mexican consular officials did not demand full identification for all those requesting the new card. There was a reason for this: most undocumented Mexicans in the United States . . . have no documents.

There is no national identification document in Mexico, like in France or Chile or Spain; although since 1994 the Federal Election Institute's voting registration card is beginning to function as one, in a similar vein to the role driver's licenses play in the United States, citizens of Mexico even in Mexico have no obligatory, universally accepted way of proving their nationality, name, address, etc. But whatever partial or make-shift documentation they may have is quickly disposed of on crossing the border, in compliance with the coyote's instructions. Getting caught with documents, particularly authentic ones, is perilous; it allows the Border Patrol to enter the migrant's name and coordinates into the INS, now Homeland Security, database as someone who committed a misdemeanor; in the future, that can mean trouble. Consequently, Mexicans in the United States have nothing: no identification from either country, no photo ID, no name, no number, no address; they live in a legal limbo, without registry in a registered world. They desperately need and want something, anything, to identify themselves when challenged by the myriad American authorities that they constantly encounter on the streets, at work, on buses and subways, in bars and concert halls or stadiums, etc. This is why we decided to do what we could to help.

In 2000, the next-to-last year of the old ID, 528,471 consular *matrículas*, as they are known in Spanish, were delivered at a nominal cost by Mexico's forty-seven consulates in the United States. In 2001, with pilot projects already operating during the last quarter in a few cities, the number increased to 695,037. But in 2002, what with the need for photo IDs growing in the United States after 9/11, and the new ID becoming available and useful, the figure skyrocketed: more than 1 million matrículas were handed out (1,190,642, to be exact), and similar numbers were reported in 2003 and 2004. By 2005, since many people had already obtained their new document, the number shrank; "only" 830,987 matrículas were distributed. By the end of 2006, nearly 6 million consular IDs were placed in the hands of Mexican nationals in the United States, and consulates in Chicago, Los Angeles, Atlanta, San Francisco, and Houston were still delivering several hundred IDs per day. It was difficult to ascertain whether by 2005–6, when the flow slackened, this was due to everyone having an ID, with new requests corresponding to new arrivals as opposed to renewals, or "old" migrants finally registering with the consulates. Similarly, other than through surveys in a handful of cities, it was impossible to determine if all ID-holders lacked U.S. documents, but in all likelihood they did. Why would anyone with a green card, which for years had allowed Mexicans to enter their country even if they did not have a valid Mexican passport, want a consular ID? But in any case the map of matrículas afforded a fascinating, detailed, and accurate picture of where Mexicans were and where they were moving. The cities with the largest Mexican communities were, as expected, Chicago and Los Angeles; the numbers for the latter were split up over the several consulates Mexico has in the Los Angeles metropolitan area (Oxnard, San Bernardino, and Santa Ana). But cities like Atlanta, Dallas, Houston, San Jose, Phoenix, and San Francisco all had distributed more than 200,000 IDs by mid-2006: Austin, Fresno, Denver, Las Vegas, New York, Orlando, Portland, Oregon, Raleigh, Sacramento, and San Diego had all delivered more than 100,000.

The actual manufacture and delivery of the IDs, however, was not the only crucial aspect of this process and policy. The "creeping legalization" approach that Mexico tacitly—and in my mind, at least, quite consciously—adopted implied transforming into purposeful policy what migrants had been doing on their own, intuitively, for years. The matrícula made it increasingly feasible. Every Mexican consul was instructed to negotiate with local banks, city officials, police departments, lawyers, etc., to persuade them to accept or "recognize" the ID as an official document. By late 2005, more than four hundred financial institutions had done so, allowing hundreds of thousands, and perhaps millions, of undocumented migrants to open bank accounts with consular IDs and tax-identification numbers (TINs), but without having to supply Social Security numbers. This enabled migrants to send home their remittances through the banking system, instead of having to rely on other, extremely onerous devices. The reduction in the cost of sending money back home dropped dramatically as a result, not only by cutting commissions from around 15 percent to less than 7 percent, but also by eliminating the wire companies' abuses on the rate of exchange (both north and south of the border). This was certainly one of the multiple explanations for the spectacular increase in remittances outlined in Chapter One.

Similarly, by June 2006, more than 1,200 police departments across the United States had accepted the consular ID; 390 city governments and 170 counties had done the same. One of the most rewarding moments of my term as foreign minister was the formal session I attended of the San Francisco city council on April 7, 2002, when mayor and former California assembly speaker Willie Brown, as cool and hip as ever in his last days in City Hall, informed me of the council's decision to recognize the matrícula as an official document for all intents and purposes of daily life. By mid-2005, more than 200,000 Mexicans, mostly from the San Francisco Mission District, possessed a consular ID, which allowed them to open bank accounts; identify themselves to police officers; get on a bus, a train, or a plane with a photo ID; pay taxes; etc.

Some states have included the matrícula in the range of documentation that applicants can use to prove identity for securing a driver's license. According to the National Immigration Law Center, currently thirteen states—Idaho, Indiana, Michigan (on a case-by-case basis), Nebraska, North Carolina, New Mexico, Oregon, South Dakota, Tennessee, Texas, Utah, Washington, and Wisconsin—allow the matrícula as an acceptable ID to obtain a driver's license. In California, the jewel in the crown, the issue became one of the burning topics of state politics after 2001, since the beginning of Governor Gray Davis's second term, and through Arnold Schwarzenegger's second campaign for governor in 2006. The California state assembly approved several bills authorizing the issuance of driver's licenses to matrícula holders even if they could not prove they were in the United States legally, but the two governors refused to sign them. Schwarzenegger, however, would probably end up accepting the principle, under certain conditions, as it became increasingly clear that in his state, being "tough" on immigration was bad politics. By March 2006, opposition to granting driver's licenses to immigrants without papers had dropped ten points: 52 percent of Californians were opposed, 44 percent in favor.

Obviously, any state that allowed its Department of Motor Vehicles to deliver licenses to consular ID holders knew it was embarking on a slippery slope. With a license, bank account, Blockbuster video-rental card, or library card and tax records, rent contracts, or an electricity contract, as well as many other similar documents, many "illegals" could begin to erase the abstract line separating legality from its opposite. After these attributes of normal everyday life in the United States were acquired, others followed: credit cards, mortgages, cell phones, setting up a small business, perhaps. In February 2007, the *Wall Street Journal* reported that Bank of America had begun offering credit cards to undocumented customers, identified as people without Social Security numbers. In fact, this had been going on for some time, the process having apparently begun in Wisconsin in 2003. Thanks partly to the matrícula and the Mexican consuls' negotiations with local banks, Mexicans had, as I have indicated, opened hundreds of thousands, if not millions, of bank accounts with small but not negligible balances. These backed up the credit cards, which were not exactly debit cards but instead something like revolving credit lines. According to information obtained directly from Wells Fargo Bank—one of the first in the country to allow accounts opened with a consular ID—between November 2001 and July 2004, Mexicans opened 400,000 accounts. Midwestern banks reported that for the same period, 80,000 accounts were opened with average balances of $2,000. Needless to say, a bank account, a credit card, and a credit history lead directly to mortgages, car loans, consumer loans, etc.

The road to permanent residence was beginning to open up, if only slightly. American immigration conservatives were in a sense right when they began, in 2004, to attack the matrícula as an instrument of backdoor amnesty; that was my intention, and I think, though I cannot state it as a fact, that it continued to be Fox's intention after I left his administration. The right-wing nativists tried to force the U.S. Treasury Department to forbid banks to open customer accounts unless they provided proof of legal-resident status and specifically attempted to declare the matrícula null and void for this purpose. The banking industry and the White House lobbied hard to stop the move, and the Senate defeated the conservative ploy in 2005.

Bush, for his part, never supported the consular ID, but the banks supported him, and he was not going to force them to forsake hundreds of millions of dollars in deposits just because a handful of cranky congressmen wanted him to. I had asked Powell back in 2002 to have the federal government "recognize" the matrícula, whatever that actually meant, as "compensation" for postponing the migration talks; I think he sincerely tried but failed. Still, the Mexican government transformed the daily life of millions of its citizens in the United States through the consular ID and the negotiations with U.S. institutions. Few things have made as much of a difference to migrants' everyday lives.

This was the focal point of the Mexican authorities' Plan B, while they waited in vain for Bush to deliver on his early promises. Fox increasingly resigned himself to concluding his term without an agreement, though in April 2006, when the Senate passed its bill in response to the House Sensenbrenner initiative, he was optimistic again on the chances for comprehensive reform. But through most of the period extending from 2004, when the divisions over Iraq finally faded, until mid-2006, the last time the two presidents held a substantive conversation, Fox always heard what had become the same old song from Bush: he had to placate his right wing in order to accomplish what both presidents and countries sought. Except that Bush placated much more than he accomplished, and by the end, Fox was disappointed, damaged, and dismayed by Bush's unwillingness to expend political capital on immigration reform. And when Bush finally did throw himself into the fray, in the spring of 2006, it was too little, too late for Fox: the Republican right had so much media and heartland support that it could neither be dismissed or convinced. Fox, however, used the opportunity generated by the "Immigration Spring" of 2006 to nudge Mexico, and mainly its political elite, toward a deeper understanding of exactly what "shared responsibility" entailed, and what Mexico would have to do in order for any immigration reform and/or agreement to become truly meaningful.

In February 2006, the Mexican executive branch and the Mexican Senate held a series of meetings with academics, former policy makers, journalists, and social activists to flesh out a common stance on the immigration issue. The encounters were convened under the somewhat pompous theme of "Prospects and Design Platforms for the Construction of a Mexican Migration Policy," and on March 20 their results were published in full-page ads in every major newspaper in Mexico and in the United States. While much of the text was made up of traditional Mexican official staples or bromides, some extremely bold and far-reaching statements were included in the document, particularly in regard to the pledges Mexico was willing to make in case comprehensive immigration reform took place, in consonance with the McCain-Kennedy bill outlined in the previous chapter. The joint executive-legislative pronouncement acknowledged that the migration phenomenon has international implications that demand from Mexico actions and international commitments—in particular with neighboring regions and countries—which should be guided by the principle of shared responsibility. This was the logical consequence of what Fox had announced at the very beginning of his administration: it probably marked the definitive end of Mexico's ostrichlike policy of no immigration policy. The statement subsequently recognized that Mexico must develop and enforce its migration laws and policy with respect for the human rights of all migrants and their relatives, notwithstanding their nationality and migration status. This was in response to the valid, age-old recrimination by human rights groups and Central American governments that Mexico treated "their" migrants as shabbily—or even more so—than the way the United States treated Mexicans.

The document then proceeded to formulate a series of recommendations, again some of them merely platitudes (Mexico should promote economic and social development in order to encourage people to stay in Mexico; it could hardly seek the contrary), but there were also several substantive ones, accompanied by a number of original and courageous, specific suggestions. The most important ones were the following:

> If a guest country [meaning, in translation from traditional Mexican doublespeak, the United States] offers a sufficient number of appropriate visas to cover the biggest possible number of workers and their families, which until now cross the border without documents because of the impossibility of ob-

> taining them, Mexico should be responsible for guaranteeing
> that each person that decides to leave its territory does so fol-
> lowing legal channels . . . Mexico would [thus] be in a better
> position to exhort potential migrants to abide by the proper
> rules, and to adopt measures . . . to reduce undocumented mi-
> gration. . . . It [could] promote the return and adequate rein-
> corporation of migrants. . . .

The syntaxes and English leave much to be desired, but, in a nutshell, what the Mexican establishment was affirming, at long
last and more or less explicitly, was that if a sufficient number
of guest-worker slots were provided, Mexico would deter, dissuade, or discourage a persistent or permanent illegal flow over
and beyond the legal one. Similarly, it would actively promote
the return of guest workers, participate in the design, management, supervision, and evaluation of a guest-worker program,
and even acknowledge that the success of such a program depended on the reestablishment of circularity, as well as the development of incentives that encouraged migrants to return
home. The document actually used the (modest) example of
strengthening tax-deductible housing programs in Mexico, so
that migrants could build a house in their home communities
while they worked in the United States.

The remarkable thing about this statement of purpose,
which was clearly crafted and published in order to weigh in on
the debate then under way in the United States, was that for the
first time in circles beyond the very close-knit group of presidential, foreign ministry, and interior ministry senior officials,
an exact definition of "shared responsibility" was attempted.
Granted, it was effected in euphemistic and abstract terms,
and many careful readers of the document could rightly argue

that it obligated no one. But the three fundamental questions involving the Mexican quid pro quo in any immigration agreement or comprehensive reform were finally addressed. They were, in order of importance, what would Mexico do to limit undocumented migration, and apply its own laws, if and when a deal was cut with its neighbor? Would Mexico bite the bullet and actively discourage illegal crossings into the United States, or not? Third, would Mexico co-administer and be equally responsible for a TWP? Incredibly, although Article 11 of the Mexican constitution guarantees everyone the free right of circulation, exit, and entry within, to, and from Mexico, Articles 11 and 78 of the standing General Population Law (the implementing legislation) assert unambiguously,

> The international transit of people through ports, airports, and land borders can only be carried out at points designated for that purpose and with the cooperation of immigration authorities. . . . Individuals seeking to leave the country are obliged, in addition to complying with general immigration requirements, to insure the following: identify themselves and provide to the relevant immigration authorities . . . proof that they can comply with all the requirements that, in order to enter the country they are seeking to enter, are called for in the laws of that country.

What would Mexico do, if and when an agreement was forged with the United States, to encourage temporary workers going north to come back, and eventually stay in Mexico? And what would Mexico do, in the context of a hypothetical TWP, to administer and supervise such a program, again simply applying its own laws? Articles 79 and 80 of the above-quoted legislation

explicitly defines the way in which Mexican laborers can be re-
cruited to work abroad.* These were key questions for three
sets of reasons. The first was that, as I described earlier, Mexico
had never really wanted to even contemplate any dissuasive action against illegal exits, although its own laws explicitly say
such exits are illegal. It is true, as scholar David Fitzgerald has
indicated ("Inside the Sending State: The Politics of Mexican
Emigration Control"), that between 1914 and 1918 the government of Venustiano Carranza was worried about the conscrip-
tion of Mexican nationals by the U.S. military during World War
I, and consequently accelerated an emigration-dissuasion campaign in 1919. It sought to convince potential migrants that
strong measures were being taken to prevent the exit of unhired
workers. But, as Fitzgerald laments, "in practice, this was the
bluff of a weak government without a coherent policy." According to an old anecdote, probably fictitious but nonetheless more
indicative of Mexican realities than the earlier rhetoric, Lázaro
Cárdenas, the country's most popular president of the twentieth
century, and his successor's defense minister during World War
II, when asked if he could post troops at the Tijuana/San Ysidro
border to impede Mexicans from working in the U.S. war industry illegally, snidely responded that the first to leave would be
the troops stationed on the border. Mexico simply thought—
and was probably right—that it lacked the capability to deter
people from leaving, and in addition it had no reason to do so.
This was hard, solid, unmovable Mexican official and cultural
dogma, set in stone, implying dilemmas which no one, until

---

*"In the case of Mexican workers, they shall have to prove that they
were hired for clearly determined periods of time, by a specific employer
or contractor, and with wages sufficient for satisfying their needs. . . .
The collective transfer of Mexican workers shall be supervised by officials of the Interior Ministry. . . ."

Fox, had been willing to breach; never had their modification been entertained with specific policies or measures. We shall see in the final chapter what can actually be done by Mexican authorities in this regard; it would involve excruciatingly painful decisions and trade-offs to implement.

The second compilation of reasons involved the administration of a new TWP, given still-fresh memories of the Bracero Agreement. The management of the existing TWPs—the H2A and H2B—that in 2005 included "barely" 75,000 workers, has been largely left in the hands of the state governors, U.S. consulates—essentially the Monterrey mission—and employers themselves. The Mexican federal government has proved extremely reluctant to participate in any aspect of the programs, fearing the corruption it would entail, the political cost it would have to pay, and the bureaucratic obstacles it would face. Accepting that it would now engage in the design, administration, and supervision of a much larger program (probably involving an additional 200,000 workers at the very least) represented a major about-face for Mexico, but it corresponded exactly to what senators Kennedy and McCain had included in their legislation in relation to source-country cooperation. This was particularly valid regarding Mexican cooperation in restoring and strengthening circularity, i.e., encouraging migrants' homebound return through various mechanisms. True, Carranza (again) selectively financed repatriations as a preemptive measure to avoid national humiliation; according to Fitzgerald, Mexico sponsored 50,000 repatriations during the 1921–22 U.S. recession. But this was an ephemeral approach, never replicated (with the partial exception of the Bracero era). For the very reasons just enumerated, Mexicans have been wary of new attempts at cooperation. The February 2006 document in this sense also constituted a watershed.

The third collection of reasons originated in U.S. skepticism toward Mexico's willingness and ability to deliver on promises of shared responsibility. Despite my own close—and I think, trusting—relationship with Colin Powell, I was never really able to convince him that I meant business on dissuading unauthorized emigration if we made a deal, and even less that I could comply with it. Ambassador Davidow said more openly what others thought: in a memorandum of conversation I received from my negotiator, Gustavo Mohar, relating an exchange he had with Mary Ryan from the State Department on October 30, 2001, she confided that in a meeting with a group of U.S. senators, Davidow had been "emphatic in expressing his doubts about the Mexican government's ability to fulfill the commitments that the [migration] negotiations implied, among other reasons because of the lack of coordination within the [Mexican] government." For these motives, it was absolutely paramount for Mexico to take a stand, as elliptical as it may have seemed, and step up to the plate on these matters, at a time when comprehensive immigration reform appeared imminent. Bush had promised Fox at their last direct bilateral meeting, in Santiago, Chile, in November 2005, that there would be legislation, and that he would support McCain-Kennedy or some version of it; Fox rightly decided that he needed to show the Americans that he was willing to invest political capital to achieve what he wanted.

This, together with one more challenge it set itself, was essentially what Mexico spent its time on during the interval between 9/11 and late 2005 when the migration issue heated up once again. That challenge was daunting indeed, and could not be met in a satisfactory fashion in a short period of time. It consisted in helping to organize, unify, and mobilize the Mexican communities in the United States through the creation of the

Instituto de Mexicanos en el Exterior (IME), or Institute for Mexicans Abroad, the latest in a series of programs or institutions created by the Mexican government as a link with the diaspora, or what it liked to think of as a diaspora.

Since the mid-1970s, the Mexican government had attempted to establish permanent, solid, and direct links with Mexicans and Mexican Americans in the United States. All of these efforts had worked partly, and failed for the most part. The explanation for this futility probably lay first in a misconception: Mexican-Americans (or Chicanos, Latinos of Mexican descent, etc.) did not think of themselves—nor did they want to be seen—as a diaspora. They loved Mexico perhaps, maybe conserved family in the home country, or retained their affection for Mexican folklore (not much more), but end of story. Furthermore, recently expatriated Mexicans were either profoundly apolitical or deeply distrusted the government of a country that had, in their view, obliged them to emigrate. Finally, Mexicans and Mexican Americans abroad were quite a heterogeneous group: from different states, engaged in multiple activities, with differing interests.

Be it as it may, the Fox administration thought it could overcome these obstacles of the past, and in April 2003 created the above-mentioned institute. Its origins lay in the now well-known *clubes de oriundos*, or hometown associations (HTAs), a sort of local club made up of migrants from the same state in Mexico (for example, Zacatecas in the Los Angeles area) or even from the same town. As has almost always been the case for migration flows, people from the same community in the source country end up living and working in the same community in the host country. This was especially true for the original sending states, but, as I described at the beginning of the book, it continues to be the case—for poblanos in New York, for example. This occurs on a small scale as well: for years every Mexican in Berkeley, California, came from the Jalisco town of Tepatitlán; most of the nearly 200,000 Mexicans in Minneapolis/ St. Paul were originally residents of the tiny Morelos town of Axochiapan. These clubs or associations send money home collectively—for public or social works, for example—but they also teach English, organize events northside, and engage in philanthropy. The first associations sprang up in cities like Chicago and Los Angeles, but have now spread across the United States. In 2003, there were 623 of them, mostly in California (329), Illinois (170), Texas (48), and New York (27); their members were mostly from Zacatecas, Jalisco, Michoacán, Guanaguato, and Guerrero. These HTAs have acquired an increasingly important role in the Mexican community in the United States and become one of the foundations of the IME and of the Mexican and Central American mobilizations of 2006 and 2007. They reproduce the virtues and vices of the community: solidarity, generosity, activisim, and commitment, as well as persistent, endless divisions and bickering over practically every imaginable issue.

The IME was headed by Cándido Morales, an agricultural worker from the Bay Area who, after more than thirty years in the United States, agreed to return to Mexico. The institute included an advisory board made up of 125 members, 105 of which are elected by the communities they represent. The other members come from existing Latino organizations in the United States such as LULAC, MALDEF, the UFW, and the National Association of Bilingual Education. It also comprised representatives of Mexico's thirty-two state governments. This board meets twice a year, sometimes in Mexico, sometimes in the United States, and recommends policies to the Mexican government on issues of interest and importance to the "diaspora." The IME has a series of programs—health, education, recognition, "Invest in Mexico," etc.—and the quality of its successive elections has been improving, in terms of the acceptance of their results, the number of communities and people who participate, and the legitimacy of the elected representatives. But, most important, there are reasons to believe that many of the IME leaders— some of whom spring from the "old guard," like Cándido Morales, but others who belong to younger generations—were actively involved in the spring 2006 Latino demonstrations across the United States. Many of the organizers, promoters, and activists of the anti-Sensenbrenner movement were elected members of the IME Advisory Board in 2005, and many others will in all likelihood be elected in 2008. This new Mexican attempt might actually work, if the Calderón administration sustains it and corrects the inevitable mistakes and defects that surrounded IME during the Fox term.

Could the Fox administration have done more, strictly on the migration front? Probably not. Many critics of Fox and Mexico in the United States respond that their neighbor's emphasis should be on creating jobs in Mexico, and keeping migrants at home, though this tends to negate the increasingly patent existence of an integrated labor market. Moreover, it is scarcely incompatible with achieving the best possible treatment for those who have already left, or for those who will continue to leave for a while, even if employment in Mexico starts growing rapidly tomorrow. We have already seen how linking the migration issue with U.S. security was clearly and decisively attempted, but proved futile until the Americans themselves came around. Although I was no longer in office during most of this period, I can only conclude that Mexico did what it could, perhaps being remiss in spending more money on its consulates and their local lobbying efforts and on identifying American corporations specifically interested in promoting immigration from, and in strengthening ties with, Mexico. The decisive conundrum Mexico faced, however, was that it possessed less and less leverage—almost none, in fact—over what the United States did during this same lapse.

The first thing the United States did was to keep making promises, albeit of an abstract nature: "I remain committed to comprehensive immigration reform," Bush repeated endlessly to Fox, though he also clarified that the White House had to cover its right flank, and that the Mexican government should not interfere in the debate. This begged another question for Mexico: should the Fox administration have continued to lobby the U.S. Congress and American public opinion vigorously, as it did in 2001–2, or was it right in heeding Bush's counsel and refraining from pursuing many of the tactics I resorted to during my time in office? Open and constant lobbying had placed the issue on the agenda, and discretion and prudence brought nothing; the jury is still out on this dilemma. The other question was: why did Bush keep making promises of this nature to his counterpart? Beyond his own undeniable sensitivity and understanding of the issue, the politics were inescapable. As we already stressed, the numbers were unmistakable, even if their political repercussions were far more convoluted.

In 1996, Bill Clinton obtained 70 percent of the overall Latino vote, which in turn represented 5.1 percent of the electorate. In 2000, Al Gore received 62 percent of the Hispanic vote, which rose slightly, to 5.8 percent of the total. In 2004, John Kerry dropped to 60 percent, and Bush got 40 percent of Latino votes, which now corresponded to 6.6 percent of the entire turnout. Thus, the Republican Party was steadily making inroads in an unfriendly yet growing electorate, mainly thanks to George Bush himself (a Texan, with broken but enthusiastic

Spanish), but also as a result of his attitude and discourse on immigration. If the Republicans continued along this path, especially among Latinos of Mexican origin—the fastest growing segment, as we have seen repeatedly—they could eventually establish a lock on presidential elections. Conversely, if they did not persist successfully in this endeavor, their prospects turned gloomy, particularly when the census numbers for 2003 showed that what everybody had known would occur at some point happened sooner than expected: Latinos had become the United States' largest minority, surpassing African Americans. The perfect counterfactual example could be found, of course, in the Republican debacle of 2006: in that year's midterm elections, the GOP obtained only 30 percent of the Hispanic vote (back to where they were in 1996), but, more important, the Latino share of the total electorate had jumped to 8.6 percent. No one doubted that the reason for this Republican regression lay in the strident anti-immigrant stance that conservative Republicans in the House had staked out in the spring and summer before the election.

In fact, the evolution was even more grim if one looked closer at the two largest Mexican-Hispanic states, California and Texas. In the first state, in 1996, Clinton conquered 85 percent of the Latino vote, which represented 11.7 percent of turnout. In 2000, Gore got 73.5 percent of the Latino electorate, which had grown to 13.9 percent of the total. But in 2004, Kerry fell back to 66 percent, and Bush rose to 32 percent, the highest ever of a rising turnout: 16.2 percent. The bad news was that in the 2006 midterms, with the same large participation (16 percent), Republicans fell back to 28 percent. In Texas, it was the same story. In 1996, Clinton received 84.3 percent of a 17.1 percent Latino share of the total vote; the numbers for 2000 were 65.7 percent for Gore (much less, logically, with favorite son Bush on the ballot, who got 32 percent of an 18.6 percent Latino turnout). But in 2004, the Republicans kept on improving: Bush rose spectacularly, to 49 percent of the Latino electorate or even 59 percent, according to some exit polls; turnout grew to 19.3 percent. But in 2006 it was back to basics: the GOP was slammed, regressing to 33.2 percent, the same as Bush in 2000, with a turnout of only 16.5 percent.

George Bush continued to talk the talk during those years. The only issue on which Democrats and Republicans, liberals and moderate conservatives, coastal states and the hinterland, young and old could agree that the American president at war was speaking sensibly on was immigration. He obviously did not convince everybody, particularly in his own party, and many Democrats refused to acknowledge his compassion and conviction in this field. Until early 2006, he did not really address the contradiction implicit in his own stance: wanting to establish a legal avenue for people to enter the United States, but refusing to confront the issue of the status of those already in the United States.

His address on January 21, 2004, from the East Room of the White House, proposing a guest-worker program, was one of the more substantive, compassionate, and eloquent speeches he delivered during his first term. First, he stressed the contribution immigrants make to the United States, specifically mentioning Mexicans, and his own upbringing in west Texas. He went on to link that heritage to the current legal situation and the broken system he wanted to fix, rightly regretting the existence of an illegal labor market, an underground economy, and, most important, millions of jobs in the United States not being filled by Americans because Americans do not want them. He could have added, of course, that Americans don't want them because of the wages, but if employers paid Americans acceptable wages, the jobs would leave the country. And he acknowledged, "Yet these jobs represent a tremendous opportunity for workers from abroad who want to work and fulfill their duties as a husband or a wife, a son or a daughter." No speech, however heartfelt and sensitive, made by any president, is drafted without polling and focus groups; Bush seemed to be following the polls on this particular facet of the issue, since many surveys in 2004, and even more so in 2006, showed that up to two-thirds of Americans think immigrants take jobs Americans don't want, instead of taking jobs away from Americans.

Bush showed he grasped the tragedy that migrants experience, and the pain and danger they have to face in order to simply fill a job no one else will do: separating from their families, walking through the desert, living in the shadows, becoming victims of polleros. But though he said many of the right things, he didn't draw the right conclusions from them. He insisted on the security question, but more than three years after that speech, it remains unclear both to U.S. authorities and experts how exactly, at an acceptable cost and with existing technology and diplomatic constraints, the United States can "secure its border." He was also unable to avoid the pitfalls of the "whole enchilada": the American economy needs foreign labor, it should be allowed in, but those who already entered unlawfully should not be rewarded. How so? And those who do come should go home after they finish their work. So which is it? Will the United States need more or less foreign labor in the future?

Bush, like many before him, attempted to finesse the contradictions in his discourse. He wanted temporary workers to come to the United States but return home when they finished, supposing they ever did. He wanted to generate various incentives for this to happen but refused to create them for those who could have access to the program and were already in the United States, continuing to oppose amnesty and a path to citizenship, though he did propose an increase in the number of green cards. So the question remained the same: Why would anyone already in the United States leave voluntarily to line up interminably in Mexico? Just because the American president announced he would try to increase the number of green cards? The subsequent "turnstile" theory of having people leave and enter on the same day, at a given point of entry, was severely questioned for this very reason: there was no conceivable incentive for a migrant to accept this cumbersome and unlikely path to citizenship. Finally, Bush focused on a crucial aspect of any program that Republicans generally prefer to ignore tacitly—labor rights, laws, and enforcement—almost explicitly rejecting any analogy with the Bracero Agreement: "This new system will be more compassionate. Decent, hardworking people will now be protected by labor laws, with the right to change jobs, earn fair wages, and enjoy the same working conditions that the law requires for American workers."

Unfortunately, Bush dropped the ball on most of these matters. He did not have his own people in the government flesh out the details of his proposal; he did not work from the outset to help senators McCain and Kennedy obtain the Republican support they needed for the legislative translation of this remarkable speech; he did not persuade the fanatics on his right that rejecting this plan would weaken him, his party, and his friend and neighbor in Mexico; he did not distract himself sufficiently from Iraq—perhaps understandably—to infuse this issue with the same passion and intensity that he devoted to others. He allowed his right wing to dominate the agenda, and, unless major reform takes place during the first semester of 2007, he will be remembered in Mexico, and by many Latinos, as "el presidente del muro": the man who tried to build the wall.

On October 26, 2006, in a ceremony at the White House, George Bush signed the hateful Secure Fence Act, which authorized the construction of seven hundred miles of fencing along the border with Mexico, as well as more vehicle barriers, checkpoints, and lighting to help prevent unauthorized entries. It entrusted the Department of Homeland Security to increase the use of advanced technology such as cameras, satellites, and unmanned drones to reinforce border infrastructure. Bush said that this was only part of his efforts to reform the immigration system, that there was more to do: enforce the laws on employers hiring illegals by reinforcing document verification and combating identity theft and forgery, create a TWP (again), and face the reality of those already in the United States. While still opposing amnesty, Bush finally accepted that there was a rational middle ground between an automatic path to citizenship for every undocumented migrant and mass deportation. For the nth time, he placated the right, arguing that securing the border was the only way to achieve comprehensive reform.

But all that came of this futile and Byzantine strategy were further concessions to the anti-immigration lobby and no reform. The fence drew criticism everywhere: from the pope's balcony in Rome to Mexico's new president, from the governments of most Latin American countries to the United Nations. It was one more cherry on the worldwide cake of anti-Americanism, or anti-Bushism, increasingly extrapolated into resentment against the United States and no longer just its president and his policies. The right did not give that president his guest-worker program, and his party received a vicious drubbing in the midterm elections a week after the signing. Everyone knew the fence would never actually be built, since Homeland Security did not actually believe in it, Congress did not actually appropriate sufficient funding for it, and the obstacles in its way, ranging from environmental impact studies to protect coyotes (the animal kind), hares, spiders, and snakes, along with serious reservations by inhabitants of reservations along the border scheduled for fencing, would tie it up indefinitely. But it became a symbol of American duplicity and hypocrisy, and of Mexican humiliation, once again. Bush would have been better served by vetoing it and using it as a foil for combating racism, demagogy, and imaginary solutions to real problems.

After the Republican defeat in the November 2006 elections, George Bush, as we know, began searching for an exit strategy from Iraq. There may be a military or political one available somewhere, but it appears unlikely that the man who invaded Iraq can ever vindicate himself in the eyes of the rest of the world. The United States will, of course, regain its prestige, credibility, and respect abroad; that is just a matter of time. Bush will not, even if he were to sign a major, generous, well-crafted immigration reform bill before he leaves office. The paradox is that it could have been different. Immigration would never have constituted a forceful enough antidote to the venom of indignation that Iraq has generated throughout the world. But it could have cast Bush in a somewhat different light. I recall a half-hour one-on-one conversation with British prime minister Tony Blair when he visited Mexico in August 2001. On our helicopter ride to a British-made oil rig in the Sound of Campeche, he asked me how the immigration talks were going, probably as the result of a relevant article in *The Economist*; this was a fortnight before Fox's trip to Washington. I rapidly summarized where we were, and vividly remember his response: "Practically every developed country faces an immigration dilemma; many of the developing countries do. If the United

States and Mexico can reach a long-term agreement on this, it will become an example for all the countries, rich and poor, who have to tackle the same problem. It could become a symbol of the new type of relationship that can be built between rich and poor countries. I hope you and the Americans are successful." At the moment, we were not.

EIGHT

What can be done in the short, medium, and long term? As we have seen throughout these pages, there are no simple answers to complex, delicate, and, on occasion, intractable problems. Nothing on the immigration front ever is devoid of costs, pain, and tough decisions; and nothing ever happens quickly. With time, perhaps in ten to fifteen years, when the Mexican population stabilizes at around 135 to 140 million inhabitants (possibly a bit less if the birth rate continues to plummet), and U.S. demand for low-wage, low-skill labor also evens out, many of the conflictive facets of the issue may simply fade away, though Mexican migration's multicausal, multifactor origins and persistence suggest that caution and skepticism are in order. The sum of elements that have driven migration for more than a century cannot be boiled down to one single, economic consideration. In addition, however, even if the issue were to attain manageable, reasonable dimensions, given the growing integration of the two economies and societies, problems will remain: assimilation, right of and obligation to return, remittances, exclusion and racism, double nationality and double loyalty, cultural "intrusion" and "blowback," and many others. If history elsewhere is any lesson, migratory flows eventually do come to an end, although they have not in the case of Mexico after more than a century of existence. The Spanish and Portuguese eventually ceased traveling to northern Europe once their economies prospered, wage differentials shrunk, and others filled the job vacancies they once sought. The same happened with Koreans in Japan, and, to a lesser extent, Turks in Germany. But even if these precedents finally do apply to Mexico and the United States, that promised land still remains beyond the horizon. In the meantime, something has to happen, even if the something is nothing, that is, the perpetuation of the status quo.

Before examining the two realistic options for the future, we must dispose of the quick fixes that understandably many observers and actors are so fond of. The first quick fix is the most obvious one: ideally, the Mexican economy would begin to grow between 5 and 6 percent yearly, creating around 1 million jobs per year, in other words, some 250,000 less than the total of new annual entries into the labor force. Demographer Frank Bean has phrased this view succinctly:

> The number of people looking for employment in Mexico each year might stop growing and perhaps shrink sometime between 2010 and 2015. Moreover, if economic growth in Mexico were to reach the attainable but not unrealistic level of about 6 percent each year, the number of jobs could roughly equal the size of the workforce by 2010, a circumstance that has not held in the country for as long as anyone can remember . . . [but] optimistic projections about job growth seem unlikely to be realized." (*The New Americans: A Guide to Immigration Since 1965*)

While this would not, in and of itself, eliminate the migratory "push" present in Mexican society, with time it would diminish it, particularly once, after five years or so, this rate of job creation began to exert upward pressure on wages. Can the Mexican economy expand at such a pace? In principle, yes. It did so, actually surpassing this goal, between 1940 and 1980; another Latin American nation, Chile, has done so now for almost twenty years, and many of the obstacles to growth in Mexico have been suppressed in recent times. Nonetheless, it is worth stressing that between 1996 and 2006, the best ten consecutive years Mexico has enjoyed since the 1960s, the average rate of growth was barely 3 percent, just half of what is considered necessary for the number of jobs to match the number of workers. In 2007, the figure will be slightly less than 3 percent.

Moreover, if this were to occur, it would not affect the "pull" side of the equation: the apparently insatiable American demand for low-skill, low-wage labor. The salary differential being as wide today as it is, many experts feel that it would take years of high growth in Mexico and diminishing demand in the United States for any significant impact on immigration to materialize. At the end of the day, migration will begin to slacken when the newly arrived start needing much more time to find a job, and eventually realize that none are available, at least not at a wage level that makes the entire effort and torment worthwhile. In principle, even on immigration issues markets will clear . . . eventually. When will Mexicans cease coming to the United States? When they stop finding jobs quickly enough, at sufficiently attractive wages, and start having to overcome such adverse obstacles that it will no longer be worth their while. Theoretically, that day will come: either because U.S. demand for Mexican labor loosens, or because the wage differential between the two nations diminishes, or because fences, walls, raids, deportations, and outflow regulation make the crossing much more dangerous and expensive. This all will happen one day, as it has, in some fashion or another, in every other case, even though the Mexican one is special, as I have tried to explain. That point is far away on the horizon, and thus the type of time frame it involves takes us directly to the demographic factor: only when the pool of potential emigrants begins to dry up will migration truly slow down. So the apparent solution, often pointed to on the right in the United States and on the left in Mexico—solve the problem by wishing it away, thanks to enhanced economic performance by the sending country—is either imaginary in the short run or redundant in the long term because it will happen anyway.

President Felipe Calderón has scored valuable debating and propaganda points insisting on his approach to the out-migration challenge by attracting investment in Mexico and creating jobs locally. He is, of course, absolutely right, just as practically all his predecessors were when they said the same thing. The problem is that even if this were to occur, as it did under José López Portillo between 1978 and 1988 or under Carlos Salinas between 1990 and 1993, migration continues, growth is neither sufficient nor sustainable, and previously existing realities do not vanish. In the long term, this is what should and probably will happen; but we are still far removed from that long term.

The other quick fixes are equally far-fetched. Building a wall or a succession of fences to keep Mexicans out, while possibly feasible today—in contrast to previous times—thanks to improved technology, a broadening U.S. constituency for a hard-line approach and lower costs of implementation, remains unrealistic. The outcry in Mexico and Central America, the sums involved—even if they are smaller than before—and the damage to the United States' already tarnished image throughout the world make this idea unworkable as a full-fledged definitive solution. In addition, there is no guarantee it would succeed: so far fences and walls have not made a dent in immigration, and there is little reason to believe they will, in the larger scheme of things. No one can absolutely discard the possibility that enough miles of fencing, high-tech devices, rapid-deployment Border Patrol forces, and enormous increases in the number of the latter could bring down the levels of unauthorized entries for a while. But it seems highly dubious that this could be either long-lasting or sustainable, in view of the above-mentioned considerations. That does not mean that the U.S. government will not attempt—indeed, it is already trying—to shut down the border as much as it can. The Secure Border Initiative (SBI), launched in 2005, and the SBInet procurement program and contract—awarded to the Boeing Corporation in September 2006—go in this direction. These efforts include an increase in the number of Border Patrol agents by 6,000 for 2008, bringing the total number of Border Patrol agents to more than 18,000, doubling the number of agents working when Bush took office. The government's objectives for the SBInet program, according to testimony before Congress in February 2007, are to: "detect an entry when it occurs; identify what the entry is; classify its level of threat (who the entrant is, what the entrant is doing, how many, etc.); respond effectively and efficiently to the entry, bringing the situation to an appropriate law-enforcement resolution. These requirements are enduring and fundamental to the task of securing the border at and between ports of entry." It provides for the construction of 70 miles of fencing in 2007 and 110 miles in 2008: practically nothing in terms of deterrence, and certainly nothing close to the magnitude of the outrage that the fence has generated, but nonetheless a signal of what is to come. Furthermore, the fence leaves untouched the problem of what to do with those who got in before it was built: the 12 or now 13 million individuals without papers currently in the United States. And last, the fence omits the gate question: Will there be doors in it? Who will be allowed to enter through those doors? For how long? Are they "enter only" gates or multipurpose exit and entry gates?

Similarly, threatening or contemplating the deportation of 12 million people living in the shadows is both illusory and inconceivable. Illusory, because the estimated cost of each detection, arrest, and deportation is approximately $20,000, making the total expense upward of $250 billion; inconceivable, because the United States—and the world—of Operation Wetback is not the United States of today. The internal and international clamor that such a move would provoke makes it unthinkable. This, of course, without even considering the legal ramifications (can American-born children of unauthorized migrants be deported?), the reaction against the roughly 1 million Americans who reside in Mexico, and the impact on the U.S. economy. It would adjust after a while, but how long and how painful would it be?

In fact, there are only two realistic avenues of evolution for the migration conundrum. One, the traditional approach, probably the one the current Mexican administration and perhaps even the powers that be in Washington would prefer, is to leave well enough alone. In this view, with strengthened border enforcement by the United States on the Mexican border and by Mexico on the Guatemalan border; through free trade and theoretically ensuing economic growth for Central America and the Dominican Republic; and improved economic performance in Mexico;

and enhanced interior surveillance in the United States (combating identity theft, establishing the equivalent of a national ID card, toughening and applying employer sanctions), total new illegal entries can be brought down to fewer than 500,000 per year (a bit more than half what they probably are now). The 12 million undocumented already "out of the barn" will eventually be assimilated throughout the United States; they represent, after all, only 4 percent of the population and the fact they are now spread out makes things more difficult in the short term but facilitates them over time.

For Mexico, this answer helps it avoid having to make tough choices on domestic enforcement of any bilateral agreement. It guarantees a minimal and acceptable safety valve, as perilous and costly as the crossing might get, and ensures that remittances will continue, at least for a significant interval. This is ultimately what Mexico has pretty much been doing for the last century, based on its difficult-to-contradict conviction that the U.S. economy and society need Mexican labor, and will need it more and more, not less and less. If this premise holds, Washington will not really close the border, whatever hysterical rhetoric and strident threats some American lawmakers may spout, since economic considerations will keep it open by force. In this view, there is no downside for Mexico in sustaining the status quo, and there are many risks implied in any of its conceivable transformations, even supposing the United States were actually to embark on major immigration reform with Mexican cooperation.

Likewise, for the United States, this option is not unattractive. It also allows the United States to evade heartrending, unpleasant choices; it permits ploys and tricks to placate the extremes (a make-believe fence for the right, clamping down on cheating employers for the left); and it makes no one too unhappy. Conservatives can justifiably pursue their ranting and raving, unafraid that their antics will actually be taken seriously; liberals can equally maintain their stances without having to confront the inevitable consequences of their wishes, since they will never come true. Cheap labor will remain cheap; the security risk is minimal, as we saw; Democrats will recruit Hispanic citizens' votes, but there won't be that many available. Republicans will forsake them, but if they can find candidates with prestige in the Latino community—like George W. Bush in 2000 and either John McCain or Rudy Giuliani in 2008—they will manage. And Mexico, together with the other sending countries, will also survive: beyond tragedies here and there, and protests and flag-waving now and then, remittances and safety valves will justify almost any mistreatment or national offense.

There are, of course, disadvantages. Continued and accentuated dispersion will generate more and more backlash, at least for some time. The border will become increasingly militarized and conflict-prone, creating greater probabilities—and thus more certainty—of tragic and violent incidents. They can become especially odious and cruel, like many of the ICE and Homeland Security raids that began to proliferate in migrant communities across the United States in late 2006 and the first half of 2007. Some were particularly notorious, such as the one that led to the arrests of several hundred Guatemalans in a New Bedford, Massachusetts, military clothing plant who were then transferred to a temporary detention center close to the Mexican border. Many had children, American-born or not, who were forcibly separated from their parents; many had spouses who never knew what had happened. In most cases they were deported back to Mexico from the detention center. ICE and Homeland Security claim that abandoning the old "catch and release" policy has led to a significant drop in unauthorized entries into the United States, and that the raids are not directed at "illegals" but at perpetrators or users of identity theft. It seems difficult to believe and in any case remains unjustifiably harsh. If the practice is a ploy to placate the right on the eve of immigration reform, it might make sense; but the pain inflicted on children will not be easily repaired. The more successful entry curtailment becomes, the greater the cost of circumventing it and the larger the profits to be made in people smuggling: organized crime will get further involved and more tightly linked to the drug business. The mobilization of Latino communities, as happened in the spring of 2006, will put pressure on local authorities and influence electoral behavior in certain constituencies. Finally, the number of illegal immigrants will rise before it starts to taper off through assimilation, creeping legalization, demographics, and economic growth in the south. By 2015 there may well be 20 million unauthorized foreign residents in the United States. Yet this remains the path of least resistance, the road best-traveled, and the least stormy waters everyone can live with, however numerous and troublesome the squalls on the way.

There is another choice, with a small but sufficient window of opportunity, a chance that can be seized before the 2008 election, or just after it, if every actor involved perceives that boldness and vision are preferable to muddling through. This route entails serious sacrifices by both countries, as well as lacerating trade-offs, but it also holds the promise of undeniable benefits at every juncture. Its characteristics have already been described, so I will simply summarize them here, and, most important, review the concessions each party would be obliged to make, together with the long-term trends that would probably take hold. The choice essentially implies an immigration agreement between the United States and Mexico that would be extended either simultaneously or somewhat later to other sending countries, chiefly in Central America, with specific commitments and internal reforms, as well as precise terms of cooperation on the issue. Whether it starts as a bilateral deal with domestic implications or as reforms at home with bilateral corollaries is immaterial from this perspective; only the end result matters. Let's start with Mexico.

For my country, such an understanding and accord requires a series of steps that until now Mexico has been unwilling to take. The first one is to apply the law: no one should be allowed out of the country if the proper and respective procedures in the standing legislation are not complied with. If this means stopping people from leaving across the desert, so be it. Let no one be naive about this: it has been done in the past. The most recent instance, to my knowledge, was the summer of 2001, when President Fox ordered the armed forces to patrol the routes across the Sonoran Desert and impede the flow of people during the worst days of heat to save their lives and health. The tactic worked: the number of deaths dropped significantly. What really counts here is the political will and the stated intentions: it would be equally naive to suppose that Mexico has the capability to deter hundreds of thousands of potential migrants of its own, and from other countries, but it certainly possesses the capacity to try. It has not, and it will have to if there is to be any deal.

Second, Mexico will inevitably be forced to implement a series of measures in the main sending communities—which have been clearly identified, thanks to the flow of remittances through the banking system—to staunch unlawful departures at the source. These measures are of a double nature: rewards for staying, penalties for leaving. The latter can be of several types. They could include, for example, doubling the welfare stipend (known as Oportunidades, a sort of food-stamp program delivered in cash to mothers but linked to their children being in school and having their vaccination certificates current) if the male head of household is present at each monthly payday. Another possibility would be a priority slot for male heads of family present in the communities in the waiting list for mortgages, public housing, tax breaks, high-school scholarships, payment exemptions for the new health care system known as Seguro Popular, or even micro-financing for starting a small business.

The penalties are largely the mirror image of the rewards and would apply to anyone who leaves outside the agreed-upon programs—and the burden of proof lies with the individual, not with the state. They would entail restricted access to all of these benefits for households whose male head, or other members, have left or cannot prove they haven't; loss of access to certain rights, such as ejido divisions or voting rights (already de facto, in part); exclusion from the following years' TWP; perhaps even some limitation of more basic social entitlements, as painful and politically unpalatable as this may seem. After all, given a program that would benefit literally millions of Mexicans in the United States and in Mexico, severely penalizing a much smaller number for jeopardizing that program or violating its laws is a perfectly justifiable step.

These measures would have to be accompanied, clearly, by economic and regional policy approaches tending toward job creation, education, and professional training. Micro-targeting is an arduous and thankless task here: it is always hard to ascertain whether the right people receive the intended benefits and if the policies are truly generating the expected results. Still, there are such well-circumscribed sending areas of Mexico that programs directed at them should logically dissuade migration, although they might, in the medium run, encourage migration in other regions, eager to obtain the same benefits for deterring mi-

gration. And finally, there should be a clear incentive for returning from the United States and exiting the program: again,
mortgages, scholarships, tax breaks, micro-financing, improved
health services, and enhanced antipoverty program eligibility.
These incentives must also include, as I shall describe below, a
firm commitment by the government of Mexico to preserve the
citizenship of those Mexicans who, under a new TWP, will come
and go, restoring at least a modicum of circularity. This implies
voting and other social rights, access to schools, health care,
etc. This is a key component of any vision for the future.

Last, and unavoidably, Mexico has to secure its southern
border. It is a sieve that must be sealed for Mexico's own purposes and security, but also as part and parcel of any conceivable deal with its northern neighbor. If Mexico does not do it, it
is increasingly likely that the United States will do it in its place,
acting in Guatemala and Belize, countries that are much less
capable of resisting Washington's pressure for highly intrusive
forms of "cooperation" than Mexico is. George Bush's most recent swing through Latin America, early in 2007, was about
many things, but one issue was clearly joint U.S.-Central American efforts to crack down on organized crime. That's a code
word for securing Mexico's southern border from the outside.

It is not simply an immigration question. Mexico's frontier
with Guatemala is mostly a nonpatrolled river, a theoretical line
in the jungle, and a passageway for absolutely everything—
contraband, drugs, gangs, migrants, arms, precursor chemicals—
in both directions. It has always been this way, but the situation
has seriously deteriorated over the past decade. Successive Mexican governments have attempted to build highways, bridges,
and crossing points along the border, some with more fortune
than others, but by and large there is a virtual right of free passage from Guatemala to Mexico. On occasion Mexico cracks

down on the migratory flows farther north, chiefly at the Tehuántepec Isthmus choke points, but very quickly it becomes business as usual.

Some of the migrants come to work during the coffee harvest in Chiapas, and have been doing so for decades. Others—the majority—head north, on perilous train rides, in flatbed trucks, and on overcrowded buses, braving the extortion of Mexican authorities as well as the intrinsic dangers of their journey. They come largely from Central America, but also from Cuba, Ecuador, Peru, and on occasion even from Africa and Asia. Mexico deports hundreds of thousands a year, but at least an equivalent number make it to the northern border and the United States. If the practically open frontier with Guatemala was penetrable only for migrants, the case could perhaps be made that Mexico should play the same game the United States does: look the other way, permit people to come through, and in any case, let the Americans solve the problem in their country. But the damage to Mexico generated by this sieve stretches well beyond migration: the corruption and violence the situation in the area provokes has become unsustainable and much more pernicious for Mexico than just a migration dilemma.

At the same time, one of the most frequent and logical objections to any legalization of Mexicans in the United States has been that it would be a never-ending story: after all, once the unauthorized Mexicans were regularized, and every Mexican newcomer was placed in the new temporary program, Central and South Americans would build on the precedent and march north in untold numbers, unless they were also partly fitted into the new program, and partly deterred from migrating by Mexico, the point of entry. So, for reasons of its own, and in order to make any deal with the United States feasible, securing the southern border for Mexico is a must, a sine qua non or deal breaker with Washington. Indeed, many experts believe that the current numbers (250,000 deportations from Mexico, without counting those from the United States, just in 2006), together with demographic trends—Central American population growth rates remain stubbornly high—make this option an especially arduous and improbable one.

But all of these tough, agonizing Mexican decisions can only take place if they are, precisely, part of a deal. They must be part of what trade negotiators call a "single undertaking": nothing is on the table until everything is on the table. Americans could well say: Mexico should do all of this anyway, regardless of any quid pro quo with the United States. That will not fly, and this is exactly the reason why Mexico should not even contemplate any of these concessions if they are not directly and explicitly linked to their American equivalent. Which is why defining that equivalent is crucial, even if most of its characteristics have already been fleshed out during the course of this book. Now it's the United States' turn.

First, there has to be a simple, expedited, and generalized process of legalization of Mexicans—and others—in the United States today. Conditions can be set: fines for having broken the law; back taxes paid when they have not been paid already (in fact, most Mexican pay taxes); the absence of a criminal record or real security considerations (not like so many false alarms since 9/11); an English-language learning process, which cannot be equated with full proficiency *ex ante*; proof of employment and a certain "substantial presence" in the United States for a given period, although any attempt to exclude the recently arrived from the process will only create new problems—family divisions, document forgery, a new cohort of unlawful migrants waiting in line for the next legalization. The point is that those who are in the United States be allowed to stay, and, if they so desire, to become American citizens over time. The corollaries to this, obviously, consist of establishing exclusively legal channels for future Mexicans to enter, and significantly ratcheting up the cost and difficulty of doing so illegally. That means a TWP that provides enough slots to approximately include all who can find jobs in the United States today; a path to citizenship for those who want it, but with a clear indication by both countries that this is not the preferred solution; and tightening employer sanctions, identity verification, and penalties on both sides of the border for violating the letter and the spirit embedded in the new legislation.

The first corollary should be self-evident to the reader at this stage. Without an instrument to deal with the push-and-pull factors in the immediate future, with the supply and demand of both economies and societies, with the historical, self-feeding traditions and patterns, no public policy of any type seems conceivable for either country on this issue. The least worst option, given political and geographical realities, as well as international and binational experience, is a guest- or temporary-worker program, as distasteful as some may find it. Its features can also rather easily be drawn from history and experience. It must encompass a number of yearly recruits as close as possible to the total of those who currently migrate without authorization. It must be truly temporary, that is, allow someone to remain in the United States either for a fixed and limited period of time during the year (mainly for agricultural but also for seasonal-service occupations, such as hospitality workers in Colorado for the winter and summer), over several years, or for an entire year's work or a briefer duration. It must be portable, in other words, not bind the worker to his job, but permit him or her to move throughout the labor market if he or she needs to do so (because of layoffs, seasonal dips, or the business cycle in general). It must be labor-friendly: ensuring that at least standards applicable in the real world to American workers be extended to visitors—not more, not less. It must be efficiently, transparently, and simply administered by both countries' governments and private sectors, guaranteeing that the abuses, corruption, and mishaps of the Bracero era not be repeated. And, finally, it must provide a solution to the leakage dilemma: there will be a number of guests—probably around one-third—who in the long term will want to settle in the United States, for one reason or another. This entails the proverbial path to permanent residence and, eventually, citizenship. This is probably a deal-breaker for the U.S. coalition of Democrats and moderate Republicans that must be assembled for passage. Without the *choice* of citizenship— not the inevitable, mandatory decision to choose it—Democrats will prove unlikely to go along with any legalization process or TWP. For Mexico, this does not make or break a deal: no Mexican president could ever encourage his or her compatriots to seek the citizenship of another country, even if Mexico's government can help those who choose that road.

The second corollary is enforcement in the United States: of the law, the border, labor standards (including OSHA considerations), and antidiscrimination clauses. If there are sufficient legal slots and a broad legalization program, those outside the law should bear the brunt of the law. Employers and migrants who transgress should be punished: the former with fines or other penalties, the latter by deportation. Employers should be held responsible for verifying the authenticity of documents they require from employees, but the U.S. federal government should make that verification simple, cheap, and swift. Employees should pay a stiff price for faking it: forgery or not complying with the law on major matters is serious business. But cracking down on exploitation, discrimination, noncompliance with contracts for housing, salaries, overtime, transportation, etc., is just as serious. Some form of tamper-proof, easily verifiable national ID will in all likelihood have to be established: either a secure Social Security card, an unforgeable "green" or "white card," or an equivalent. And employers will have to be responsible for the authenticity of the documents they require and conserve in their files.

While well-intentioned, knowledgeable people on both sides of the border can honestly disagree about which of these alternatives is better-suited for their respective countries, I concluded years ago that a bold and visionary proactive approach that engages the United States is preferable for Mexico than the status quo, even supposing it could be maintained. Although many reasons led me to this conclusion, two in particular stand out. First, the only way Mexicans in the United States can eradicate the exploitation, discrimination, racism, and intolerance that they have been far too frequently victims of for more than a century is if they acquire the rights to defend themselves. No Mexican government will ever be able to do it for them; no U.S. federal or state authority will either, at least not fully and permanently. And the only way for Mexicans to obtain those rights is to legalize their residence in the United States, and the only way that can happen is if the other side of the equation—legal and temporary entry—is also dealt with. The status quo is thus, from my perspective, morally untenable: to condemn millions of Mexicans to an underclass unlawful, unprotected standing is not ethically acceptable, however remote the chances of substantially modifying this reality may be, or appear to be.

But in addition to these ethical motives of conviction there are powerful reasons of pragmatism and convenience that argue in favor of profoundly modifying the status quo, at least from a Mexican standpoint, both from a societal perspective and one of statesmanship. Those reasons are the ones I spelled out in a long essay published in Mexico in early 1995—which I only mention here to show that this is not a recently acquired or formulated thesis—that also became the conceptual foundation for the Fox administration's decision to pursue an immigration agreement with Washington, as laid out in another essay, also published in Mexico, in late 2000. Those reasons boil down to one that unfortunately seems to be increasingly corroborated by events, perhaps occurring later than I had surmised both in 1995 and in 2000. The fact is that the United States appears to have made the decision to seek to close the border, at least in part, and, worst of all, there appear to be conditions today—technological, fiscal, and ideological—that make this at least partly feasible. If Mexico does not "slip under" the fence, the technology, and the nativism, and lock in reforms that address its interests *before* the United States carries out its plans (like SBInet) even partially, it will be pushed from the best of all worlds—today, emigration without responsibility—to the worst of all worlds—tomorrow, a fenced border, limited immigration, interior enforcement, and no immigration reform. Indeed, the do-nothing option, premised on the perennial nature of the status quo, is probably nonexistent: the status quo will not last, because the United States today can change it. It is true, as many of the advocates of the passive option argue, that potent forces in American society and economics will combat the fence, interior enforcement, and immigration restrictions because they need immigration. Maybe, they claim, the United States *as a whole* does not need low-wage, low-skill immigration as desperately as many Mexicans think and many Americans lament, but there are powerful *sectors* of the American establishment that do. Who will win? It is impossible to know right now, but Mexico should not stake its future stability and the welfare of its twelve-plus million citizens currently in the United States on this roll of the dice. For these reasons also, Mexico should push hard for immigration reform, which will inevitably imply an immigration agreement.

Beyond the unavoidable details of any blueprint for the immediate future, there are three additional abstract theses that a proactive policy should include or contemplate. The first is whether the United States—and perhaps Canada, given NAFTA membership—plays a role in Mexican development through financial transfers along the lines the European Economic Community (before it became the European Union) followed with southern Italy in the 1960s; Ireland in the 1970s; Spain, Portugal, and Greece in the 1980s; and now, as the EU, with the new members from the former Eastern Europe, all with varying degrees of success. Washington can rightly respond that it is different from Europe, and that such a scheme is un-American; or it can point out that mechanisms of this sort were relevant and useful in the past, but are obsolete today. Both of these points are arguable—was the Marshall Plan un-American? is Brussels's current support for Poland contemporary or not?—but they . . . miss the point.

In order for Mexican migration to diminish one day, a necessary though not sufficient condition is economic growth in Mexico, and this cannot occur unless several basic bottlenecks are loosened, among them the establishment of the rule of law in ways recognizable by the international community; the construction of adequate infrastructure, particularly in the impoverished south and southeast of the country; and a dramatic improvement in the nation's educational system. While money will not automatically accomplish these tasks, without money they are hopeless. And though Mexico could have more money if it reformed its tax system, it still would be lacking the resources for this ambitious agenda. So if the United States really wishes to stem immigration from Mexico in the midterm, contributing real money (as Everett Dirksen used to say) to meet the three above-mentioned challenges is indispensable and paramount. An immigration package can be stitched together without this ingredient, but a far better development-and-immigration package can be assembled with it.

Second, it is highly probable, if not certain, that circularity as we knew it is a thing of the past. Mexicans are filling full-time jobs, no longer seasonal ones; they are settling farther and farther away from the border; they are either bringing their families with them or founding new families abroad; and they are increasingly able to live as Mexicans in the United States without having to return home. This is unlikely to change, even with immigration reform. What reform would bring about is a reduction in costs, danger, and oppression for those to come, but it would not necessarily entice those already in the United States to leave. The end of the familiar version of circularity probably signifies that instead of the ambiguous, hazy, and blurred continuum of identities and legal status that prevails today, a more clear-cut and explicit taxonomy of identities will have to be established. Mexicans who decide, for one reason or another, to stay in the United States should become Americans, and subsequently address the identity dilemmas of American society in whatever fashion they deem fit. They obviously will, and should, retain their family ties, their love for the home country or *madre patria*, their Mexican nationality (as they currently can), their culture, religion, and traditions. But their loyalty, livelihood, political involvement (including voting rights), and military service, if the case may be, cannot straddle the Rio Grande: it's one or the other. The United States and, to a lesser extent, Mexico, should encourage this process; however counterintuitive and politically incorrect it may appear at first sight, it is the only viable avenue in the midterm, that is, for the next quarter of a century or so.

The assimilation debate is quintessentially American, although a growing number of European countries are finding themselves forced to address it, as millions of foreigners, and in particular Muslims from Norrth Africa, the Sahel, Pakistan, and other parts of the Islamic world, seek work and prosperity in the "old world." What exactly "becoming American" signifies and implies is open to discussion, the moment one goes beyond the strictly—and admittedly decisive—legal definition. What type of assimilation do "old" Americans want, and what type do "new" Americans hope for? Do members of both cohorts all want the same thing and agree on it? Can the traditional patterns persist, or have the world, the countries of origin, and the United States itself changed so much that those now-ancient archetypes are no longer viable or functional? This debate cannot be radically dissociated from the immigration discussion, but it is a distinct debate and not a continuation of the latter. From afar, I continue to be a firm believer—though not as firm as years ago—in the French/American/Spanish approach: everyone who comes, stays, and wants to should become a citizen, like all the others; *tout le reste est littérature*, as Borges would say. And those who wish to come and go should also be able to do so, but must remain nationals of the country they come from and hope to return to. The German/Japanese *jus sangui* is not something I like, but individual preferences are largely irrelevant in this context. What matters, I think, is to clarify the blurry lines, and then revisit them with nuance, sensitivity, imagination, and generosity.

Conversely, those Mexican newcomers who hope to take advantage of a temporary program, and come and go for a while without harboring any intention of settling in the United States, should be encouraged to do just that. There will always be a greater number of wannabe returnees than of actual circular migrants; still, the final balance will be highly favorable to those seeking to spend the rest of their lives in their original communities. Mexico must do everything possible to foster this trend: providing help for returnees; facilitating their reincorporation into Mexican society; allowing them to retain their rights while abroad—from voting, schooling, food stamps, health care, and housing to professional training, re-immersion support, etc. They should remain Mexican, even if they spend part of the year, or a few years of their life, in the north. Also, by breaking the continuum from this direction, the two countries can perhaps construct a steady state that will last until when, many years from now, they are both ready to enter into a different type of cohabitation.

Which leads us to the third and final reflection. Mexico and the United States—again, Canada is also probably part of the process—have been integrating their economies and societies for years now. NAFTA both enshrined and accelerated this trend; an immigration deal will produce the same result. It is not only that almost all of Mexico's international economic intercourse is with the United States—trade, investment, tourism, remittances—and that such intercourse now represents a higher share of GDP than ever; or that 12 million Mexican citizens reside in the United States and 1 million Americans reside in Mexico. It is that both nations are beginning to look, think, and act more and more alike. Mexican culture—cuisine, music, language, religion, cinema, art, literature—is ever more present north of the border, in all segments of society. And American cultural influence in Mexico has been expanding since the 1940s, when the Mexican middle class emerged on the scene. This overall integration should lead—will lead—to some form of economic community that, in turn, like in Europe, will extend its ramifications into other spheres. This might all be very long in coming, but it seems misleading, and undesirable, to combat or escape from it. Addressing the always intricate, on occasion intractable, eternally irritating, and sometimes incomprehensible issue of immigration today may not postpone or hurry that future; it will simply make it easier for everybody.

At this writing, that is, in early May 2007, the United States—meaning the executive branch, the Congress, the Democrats and Republicans, Latinos and Anglos, business and labor—have not yet figured out what to do about immigration. Mexico hasn't either: the difference is that the decision lies much less in its hands than in those of its neighbor to the north. Negotiations between the White House, moderate Republicans, and the Democratic majority in both houses, but mainly in the Senate, got bogged down (not necessarily forever) over details that express substance and reflect deep divisions.

If amnesty remains a forbidden word and world, then the issue is how to achieve it and disguise it at the same time. Different answers were suggested, from the ridiculous (ask all the unauthorized residents to go home and wait) to the convoluted (establish a "touchback" system whereby they wait in line States-side, but cross the border for a few hours and then return once their turn comes) to the simple and expedite but too explicit (pay a fine and back taxes, possess no criminal record, and that's it, but without family reunification for those not yet in the United States, at least until citizenship, meaning thirteen years down the line), to the cruel and ineffective (the division of all illegals into groups depending on how long they have been in the United States, letting some stay and deporting the others, regardless of whether they belong to the same family).

If the question is a guest-worker program that does not imply an open-door policy, then the issue is how to guarantee that the leakages will not be excessive, that wages and working conditions will not become unacceptable for all, and that there will be an eventual path from the temporary to the permanent, from visiting status to citizenship. It is true, inevitably, that "temporary," as in "Temporary Workers Program," is not 100 percent "temporary." There is attrition: over time, if there is any type of path to residence and citizenship, a given percentage of people will follow that path. And if they do, at some point, some of their families will join them, depending on the type of preferences American immigration law has in place by then: spouses, children, siblings, parents, or some but not all of the above. But that is quite a bit down the road, as is the equivalent "chain" migration set off by those who currently live in the United States and who would be legalized. After eight years of temporary residence and another five of permanent residence, they could become citizens, and subsequently could bring some family members with them. And yes, that is "chain migration": at some point in the future, there will be more Mexicans in the United States than there are today. Except they would all be legal (which is what opponents of immigration say they want), and the U.S. economy would need them all; if it didn't, they would not find jobs. The United States currently allows in one million people per year legally; the U.S. economy hires roughly 1.5 million immigrants every year; consequently, half a million are unauthorized. If the United States permitted 1.5 million legal entries every year in the future, and put its existing house in order, with time markets will clear and everyone will be happy . . . sort of.

Moreover, Mexico would also be able to cooperate much more effectively with the United States if all of this is addressed intelligently and realistically. That does not mean that my country does not have its own immigration dilemmas to come to terms with. President Calderón, unlike his predecessor, seems to have decided that migrants are not "heroes" but rather a net loss for Mexico, that the solution lies in creating jobs in Mexico, and that his administration should not in any way interfere in the U.S. debate, since this is a U.S. issue. The three points are important, but arguable.

Is immigration a problem for Mexico? If Mexico could put an end to it overnight, either by creating jobs for everyone involved, placing the younger migrants in school, or restricting outflows, would it be better off than it is today? What kind of income would those who found jobs in Mexico actually receive? From a recent Central Bank of Mexico survey of remittance senders carried out in the United States and Mexico among "receivers," we know that 63 percent of all remittance senders make more than $1,500 per month, that 36 percent earn more than $2,000 per month, and that one-fourth of the total obtain more than $2,500 monthly, of which they send home more than $400. Even if Mexico could create 1.2 million new jobs per year instead of the 600,000 to 700,000 it generates in its best economic years, would they provide these magnitudes of income? If one recalls that the minimum wage in Mexico is approximately $300 per month and the average wage is slightly upwards of $500, one can only wonder whether Mexico truly would be better off if they all stayed home. Furthermore, almost everything families back home receive is dedicated to consumption, which means that if they did not get it, their consumption levels would drop. The President can't say all of this—diplomacy and political correctness *obligent*—but others can.

Second, it's obvious that the long-term solution to future migratory flows lies in creating jobs at home, but, as has been stated here many times, that does nothing for the 12 million who have already left, nor for the 6 million of them who lack papers. And since the above-mentioned hypothesis is obviously unrealistic—the Mexican economy can begin to create more jobs than before little by little, but not all the jobs Mexico needs every year—outflows will continue: a bit smaller, a bit bigger, a bit cheaper and safer, a bit more expensive and dangerous. This will persist for several years before it tapers off. This has all been studied and analyzed endlessly on both sides of the border. So President Calderón can score valid and important debating points by saying the solution lies in Mexico, but he is not being entirely forthright by stating it.

Finally, whether or not Mexico participates in the U.S. debate, it will be part of the U.S. debate. Anti-immigration advocates will throw everything and the proverbial kitchen sink at us, and if we don't respond our American friends undoubtedly will . . . up to a point. Immigration-reform supporters will invoke Mexican cooperation and participation—co-managing a TWP, sharing responsibility, applying Mexican laws—whether the Mexican government likes it or not and regardless of exactly how viable that cooperation and participation actually would be. The new Mexican administration cannot be faulted for not resolving this delicate and thorny issue straight off the bat, but it will have to do so at one stage or another.

There is no such thing as a perfect immigration reform or agreement, and there are conceivable outcomes that are less desirable than the alternative: the muddling-through status quo. If a hypothetical reform enhances enforcement and deportation; splits families; stipulates unworkable paths to legality, residence, and citizenship; and simply increases the number of temporary visas (H2A and H2B), it is likely that many people will consider the current situation preferable to this regression. Conversely, if the Democrats in the Congress make the White House and the Republicans look nativist and anti-Latino by forcing them to reject a sensible but unilateral and unacceptable proposal, they will roll up their score in the 2008 elections but get nothing done. And finally, if the White House, for the last and nth time, caves to the Republican right wing and finds itself unable to deliver ten Senate votes and thirty House votes in favor of a reasonable Democratic alternative, it will sustain Geroge W. Bush's popularity with his hard-core base . . . uselessly, since he is not running for office anymore, and the Republican nominee in 2008 will need some Hispanic votes if he is to have even a remote chance of winning.

Everyone wants fig leaves, but not everybody can fabricate or wear them elegantly. It seems likely, though regrettable, that politics will get in the way of policy on an issue that cries out for statesmanship because, as Nietzsche would say, "the people" are doomed to misunderstand it. So each side will in a sense bet the store on their hopes and convictions, rather than on a sensible assessment of what will happen. But if over a century of experience means anything, it shows that Mexicans will continue to go north, legally or not, safely or not, with circularity or without it, almost regardless of what the United States does. This is the least best outcome, but unfortunately, the most likely.

BIBLIOGRAPHICAL APPENDIX

For the reasons laid out in the preface, this book is largely devoid of footnotes. Nonetheless, in order to help the reader pursue his or her understanding or knowledge of the issues dealt with here, as well as to avoid any improper or unacknowledged use of the works of others, I have decided to list, with some detail, all the sources I resorted to, whether they were directly quoted or not. These include published books; publicly available documents; reports by task forces or study groups; public opinion polls; statistics; newspaper, magazine, or journal articles; official documents from the Mexican government; my own files from the time I occupied the Foreign Ministry; other internal Mexican or U.S. documents made available to me one way or another; and numerous interviews, conversations, and exchanges held over the years with relevant interlocutors.

Books:

Jimmy Breslin. *The Short Sweet Dream of Eduardo Gutiérrez.* New York: Crown, 2002.

Samuel P. Huntington. *Who Are We?: The Challenges to America's National Identity.* New York: Simon & Schuster, 2005.

Douglas S. Massey, Jorge Durand, and Nolan J. Malone. *Beyond Smoke and Mirrors: Mexican Immigration in an Era of Economic Integration*. New York: Russell Sage Foundation, 2005.

Robert Courtney Smith. *Mexican New York: Transnational Lives of New Immigrants*. Berkeley: University of California Press, 2004.

Mary C. Waters and Reed Ueda, eds. *The New Americans: A Guide to Immigration since 1965*. Cambridge, MA: Harvard University Press, 2006.

Raul Delgado Wise and Beatrice Knerr. *Contribuciones al análisis de la migración internacional y el desarrollo regional en México*. Porina: University of Zacatecas, 2005.

Victor Zuñiga and Rubén Hérnandez-Leon, eds. *New Destinations: Mexican Immigration in the United States*. New York: Russell Sage Foundation, 2006.

Essays:

Mohammed Amin and Aaditya Mattoo, "Can Guest Worker Schemes Reduce Illegal Migration?" World Bank Policy Research Working Paper 3828, February 2006.

Charles Bowden. "Exodus: Border-Crossers Forge a New America: Coyotes, Pollos and the Promised Van." *Mother Jones*. September/October 2006.

Juan Diez Canedo. "La Migración Indocumentada a Estados Unidos: Un Nuevo Enfoque." Banco de México. Document 24, June 1980.

Jorge Durand and Douglas S. Massey. "Mexican Migration to the United States: A Critical Review." *Latin American Research Review* 27, no. 2. (1992), pp. 3–42, available at http://links .jstor.org/sici?sici=0023-8791%281992%2927%3A2%3C3% 3AMMTTUS%3E2.0.CO%3B2-O.

David Fitzgerald. "Inside the Sending State: The Politics of Mexican Emigration Control." *International Migration Review,* 40, no. 2 (June 2006).

Alvaro Ochoa and Alfredo Uribe. "La Iglesia católica contra la emigración de trabajadores mexicanos." Quoted in "Emigrantes del Oeste." *La Epoca, Seminario Católico.* Guadalajara, Jalisco. Año III, no. 148, September 1920.

Reports:

"Immigration and America's Future: A New Chapter." Migration Policy Institute, 2006.

"In Search of Economic Parity: The Mexican Labor Force in Chicago" and "The State of Latino Chicago, This is Home Now." Institute of Latino Studies of Notre Dame University, 2003.

"Invisible No More: Mexican Migrant Civic Participation in the United States." Woodrow Wilson International Center for Scholars, 2006.

"Mexico–U.S. Migration: A Shared Responsibility." Instituto Tecnológico Autónomo de México and the Carnegie Endowment for International Peace, 2000.

Public opinion surveys:

"Immigration Survey." NPR/Kaiser/Kennedy School, 2004.

"Latino Immigrants Do Assimilate and Learn English." George Mason University.

"Los Sueños de los Mexicanos," parts I and II. *Este País,* November/ December 2006.

"México y el mundo: opinión pública y política exterior de México," 2006, and "México y el Mundo: Visiones Globales,"

2004. Centro de Investigación y Docencia Económicas (CIDE) and Consejo Mexicano de Asuntos Internacionales (COMEXI) and the Chicago Council of Foreign Affairs.

Several polls by the Pew Hispanic Center: "Attitudes Toward Immigration: In Black and White," April 2006; "Attitudes Toward Immigrants and Immigration Policy: Surveys Among Latinos in the U.S and in Mexico," May 2006; "Latinos and the Midterm Election," November 2006; all are available at http://pewhispanic.org.

Other polls can be found at http://www.pollingreport.com/immigration; the Gallup Poll, http://www.galluppoll.com; and, for California, the Field Poll Online, http://field.com/fieldpoll/; Robert Sampson, Jeffrey Morenoff, and Stephen Raudenbush, "Latinos Nix Violence," *Harvard Magazine*, September/October 2006; Ruben Rumbaut and Walter Ewing for the American Immigration Law Foundation and the Immigration Policy Center, February 2007.

As already mentioned, among the interviews and surveys carried out by me or my research assistants, the more important ones were those from June 2005, at Benito Juárez International Airport in Mexico City, of passengers arriving from New York on Mexicana Flight 001; I am grateful to Emilio Romano, CEO of Mexicana, for permission to carry out the interviews and for his explanation of why Mexicana scheduled its flights the way it did. The other surveys were carried out in Sasabe, Sonora, in June 2006 by researchers; I visited Sasabe on three occasions, in 2003, 2004, and 2006. I also thank Roberto González, owner and chairman of Grupo Maseca in Mexico City, as well Daniel Servitje, CEO of Bimbo, SA, for their willingness to provide data on sales, history, and development of their respective firms in the United States. The information on Televisa and Univsión comes from Univisión's Web site, http://www.univision.net/corp/es/history.jsp.

The public and private documents quoted and used (joint communiqués; reports on working visits; memoranada of conversations; cables from colleagues and aides, particularly migration negotiator Gustavo Mohar and Ambassadors Enrique Berruga and Juan José Bremer are mostly available on the Web site of the Mexican Foreign Ministry, http://www.sre.gob.mx, or on the Web site of the Mexican embassy in the United States, http://www.embassyofmexico.org. The private documents come from my files, as do the U.S. Department of State nonpapers, such as Secretary Powell's talking points "México Migration: A Proposal." Needless to say, nonpapers are by definition deniable; they are also discernible and traceable. President Bush's speeches can be found at http://www.whitehouse.gov. Finally, the data on the Mexican consular ID were kindly made available by friends in the Mexican Foreign Ministry; they can mostly be consulted on the Ministry's Web site, cited above.

In addition, several series or articles on immigration have appeared in major U.S. newspapers in recent times: *New York Times*, "New Data Show Immigrants' Growth and Reach," August 15, 2006; "Bipartisan Group Drafting Bill for a Simpler Path to Citizenship," December 26, 2006; the trilogy "Making a Life in the United States, but Feeling Mexico's Tug," "Fear for Hope in Immigrant's Furtive Existence," and "For Divided Family, Border Is Sorrowful Barrier," December 19–21, 2006; "Mr. Bush's Immigration Realism," editorial, December 21, 2006. "Mexico and the Migration Phenomenon," the Mexican government's stance on immigration, appeared in the *New York Times*, the *Los Angeles Times*, and the *Washington Post* on March 20, 2006, and can be

found at http://www.embassyofmexico.org/images/pdfs/Mexico
%20and%20the%20Migration%20Phenomenon%20%2002%2003
%202006.pdf. In the Mexican press: *El Universal*, "Vislumbran
sociedad civil migrante en EU," August 18, 2006; and *Reforma*,
"Dispara México cifra de migrantes," August 18, 2006. The views
from Middletown, Ohio, come from the *Butler County Press* and
the *Middletown Journal*.

Other quotes and references were taken from: "Rifts Among
African Americans over Immigration: Immigration Debate Ex-
poses Tensions Between Blacks and Latinos," http://laborcenter
.berkeley.edu/press/austin_may06.shtml; "Misguided Debate over
Undocumented Workers Ignores Larger Challenge," http://www
.btimes.com/News/article/article.asp?NewsID=9045&sID=3;
Migración femenina, efecto de las políticas económicas," http://
www.cimacnoticias.com/noticias/06abr/06042506.html; "Generations of diversity: Latinos in the United States," http://www
.findarticles.com/p/articles/mi_qa3761/is_199710/ai_n8769255
/pg_11; "La Garra de Chicago, el otro Tepito," http: //www.esmas
.com/noticierostelevisa/losreporteros/406644.html; "Instituto
de los Mexicanos en el exterior," IME Web site, http://www. ime
.gob.mx; "La Jornada, Articles on Riverside Incident, Apr 11,"
available at http://www.eco.utexas.edu/~archive/chiapas95/1996
.04/msg00101.html; "Mueren 7 indocumentados en la frontera
de México y EE.UU," http://www.clarin.com/diario/96/04/07/
brando.html; "Cruces en la frontera: migración indocumentada y
muertes en la frontera México-Estados Unidos," http:// www
.pdhumanos.org/libreria/libro5/nancy%20perez.pdf; "SRE: no
hay pruebas que impliquen a la Border," http://www.jornada
.unam.mx/1996/04/10/GURRIA00-PG.html; "The Kill-Floor Re-
bellion," http://www.prospect.org/web/page.ww?section=root&
name=ViewPrint&articleId=6332; "Inmigrantes llegan a los es-

tados centrales: El trabajo en las grandes carnicerias," http://
revcom.us/a/v19/920-29/920/storm_s.htm; "Unofficial sister cities:
Meatpacking labor migration between Villachuato, Mexico, and
Marshalltown, Iowa," http://www.findarticles.com/p/articles/mi_
qa3800/is_200201/ai_n9025860; "Meatpacking plants," available at http://www.answers.com/topic/meat-packing; "ICE's Swift
Plant Raids Netted Only Poor Folks Caught Up in the 'War on
Illegal Immigration,'" http://www.indybay.org/newsitems/2006/
12/17/18338265.php; "Thousands Protest in Los Angeles, Calling for New Immigration Legislation," http://english.peopledaily
.com.cn/200604/11/eng20060411_257576.html; "Driver's Licenses for Immigrants: Broad Diversity Characterizes States'
Requirements," available at http://www.nilc.org/immspbs/DLs/
DL005.htm. This is not an exhaustive list.

Next to last, but most important, we must mention the
data available at: the Mexican Migration Project (MMP), developed by the Research Department of Social Movements at
the University of Guadalajara and the Office of Population Research at Princeton University at http://mmp.opr.princeton.edu;
the American Community Survey, http://www.census.gov/acs/
www/; U.S. Bureau of the Census, http://www.census.gov;
Campbell Gibson and Kay Jung, Population Division, "Historical
Census Statistics on the Foreign-born Population of the United
States: 1850 to 2000," http://www.census.gov/population/www/
documentation/twps0081/twps0081.pdf; William C. Velasquez
Institute database on the Latino vote, http://www.wcvi.org/
latino _voter_research/polling_data.html.

Last, we have consulted with great benefit: the Migration
Policy Institute's Web site, http://www.migrationpolicy.org/; the
Manhattan Institute's Web site, http://www.manhattan-institute
.org/; the Woodrow Wilson Center for Scholars' Web site, http://

www.wilsoncenter.org/index.cfm; the International Migration Organization Web site, http://www.iom.int/jahia/jsp/index.jsp; an excellent source, the Migration Information Web site, http://www.migrationinformation.org; and the World Bank Web site, http://www.worldbank.org.

INDEX